Russian Fairy Tales Decoded

by
Tony Butcher

Grosvenor House
Publishing Limited

This book is published by
Grosvenor House Publishing Ltd
Link House
140 The Broadway, Tolworth, Surrey, KT6 7HT.
www.grosvenorhousepublishing.co.uk

A CIP record for this book
is available from the British Library

ISBN 978-1-83975-087-8

Acknowledgements

I would like to express my gratitude to Maharishi and his Guru Swami Brahamanda Saraswati for their easy and effortless techniques of transcendental meditation and the TM Sidhi programme that make self-realisation possible in the comfort of one's home; and in addition who have given me the gift of the devatas in the form of the goddess Durga and the ancient Vedic knowledge they have revived, which I have used in this book.

I would also like to thank Swami Satyananda Saraswati for allowing me to include a hymn called the *Pradhanikam* from his puja book the *Chandi Pathah* at the beginning of Marya Morevna.

I would also like to thank RusClothing.com for allowing me to download pictures of a couple of their lovely embroidered shirts.

In addition I would like to thank Russian Crafts for kindly allowing me permission to download the exact copies of the stories of the relevant titles for this book unchanged from their website, without which this publication couldn't have taken place. I would also like to thank RusClothing.com for allowing me to download pictures of a couple of their lovely embroidered shirts.

Contents

Foreword vii

Introduction 1
Forest Schools and the Mystery Religions 7
The Anatomy of a Folktale 14
Perun and Indra 25

The Stories
The Frog Princess 28
Marya Marevna 46
The Wee Humpbacked Pony 70
The Tale of Finist the Falcon 83
Wee Little Havroshechka 94
Vasilisa the Beautiful 102
The Clever Jackal 109
The Flying Ship 120
Tsarevich Ivan and Grey Wolf 133
Postscript 146

Foreword

Like many others, I only had a passing affection for folktales, until one afternoon in 1973. I had put a small period of time aside to help a 14-year-old boy named Anthony who was having trouble learning to read. He had been sent to a special school because he had caused a lot of disturbances in mainstream education and the teachers hadn't been able to cope with him. However, I didn't find him at all difficult because I was used to boys who played up to hide the fact that they couldn't read and didn't want their peer group to find out and make fun of them.

There was no such thing as remedial readers in those days, so I had picked a particular fairy story that I thought he could cope with, as he had already made some good progress in the short time he'd been at our school. He was going well without any need of outside help when I suddenly had a vision – the only one I have ever had in my life – that told me a great deal about so-called 'fairy tales'.

The vision was of an aged standing stone, standing in such a way to reveal that it had a rectangular top and four sides. A voice – I can't remember if it was audible or a thought transmission – explained the illustration to me.

It said: 'in addition to the waking, dreaming and deep sleep states there are four others. One of them is called the turiya state or transcendental consciousness. This gradually purifies the mind and is the key to achieving three additional higher states of consciousness.

Firstly, all the characters in the story are aspects of the same person. There is always a place in the story that brings about a significant change in that person that allows them to be introduced to three consecutive tasks, which will result in eternal happiness.'

It was both a bit of a surprise as this kind of thing had never happened to me before, but I took it as important and tried it out on different stories from time to time. It wasn't until many years later that I had a book published on the subject called *Yoga Consciousness in the Ancient mystery religions*, when I analysed ten of the Grimm brothers' fairy tales.

Even then I was still a bit surprised when the goddess Durga sent me a silent message to do the same for some Russian stories. I didn't know anything about Russian culture at the time, or in fact why I had been chosen.

During the course of one of my morning pujas to her she reminded me that I had a long association with stories from the distant past. She reminded me of a time when I had been really surprised at being picked to play the lead in a Teacher Training College play, even though I had never shown any interest in acting. I had been chosen to play the part of a travelling street entertainer in the Middle Ages. I had been equally surprised when playing the part at how easily I stepped into the role and also how natural it felt. The freedom of the open road had really appealed to me.

I had obviously been a storyteller and musician in one of my previous lives. Whether I had helped distort the stories to make them funnier or more dramatic is still open to question, but what I do know is that it is now my duty to restore and remind people of their original versions.

INTRODUCTION

The purpose of writing this book is to bring alive a tradition that has slept peacefully among us for a very long time. Although the modern versions of the stories are well known, the significance of the symbolism they use has been forgotten for a long time – so long in fact that all traces of the higher states of consciousness they were composed to convey have been erased.

In other words, something great has been hidden from the world. Yet all the high places of learning spread the widespread illusion that we are the cleverest, wisest and the most civilised beings that have ever lived on earth.

If one looks at what the history books tell us about the past few thousand years, it is difficult not to agree with them. But if we look at myths and early religious material, they say the opposite, namely that there was once a golden age when spirituality reigned, and not just on the level of belief but involving actual contact with the gods and acuteness of mind, coupled with the ability to perform miraculous actions that we can only 'pooh-pooh' as impossible in our time.

It seems strange that the modern western world has chosen the straight line theory of time, when philosophers from Pythagoras down to Einstein say that as space is curved, the time that moves within it must also be curved. Also Joseph (2010), in agreement with Pythagoras and George Gamow, said that: 'patterns repeat themselves in Nature from the sub-atomic to entire galaxies'.

This entirely fits what Sri Yukteswar rediscovered in modern times. Just as there are four main seasons in the year, in which the first and the fourth – – spring and winter – are complete opposites, the same is also true in a much larger wheel of time called a yuga, which is about 12,000 years long.

The larger and longer wheel of time follows a similar pattern to that of the day. During the first period of a descending yuga, the time of the golden age is well over 4,000 years, when humans' mental and emotional qualities are at 100% as compared with only 25% in a yuga's shortest period of about 1200 years.

Quoting from the laws of Manu and the *Padma Purana*, Yogananda's guru Sri Yukteswar rediscovered the truth about yugas, which had become distorted due to the fall of human awareness about 5,000 years ago. He said that one full yuga lasts 12,000 years and consists of four main periods. The breakdown of this is as follows:

<u>Dawn Era Dusk Total Name</u>

400 + 4000 + 400 = 4800 years. Satya Yuga (Golden Age)
300 + 3000 + 300 = 3600 years. Treta Yuga (Silver Age)
200 + 2000 + 200 = 2400 years. Dwapara Yuga (Bronze Age)
100 + 1000 + 100 = <u>1200</u> years. Kali Yuga (Iron Age) 12,000 years

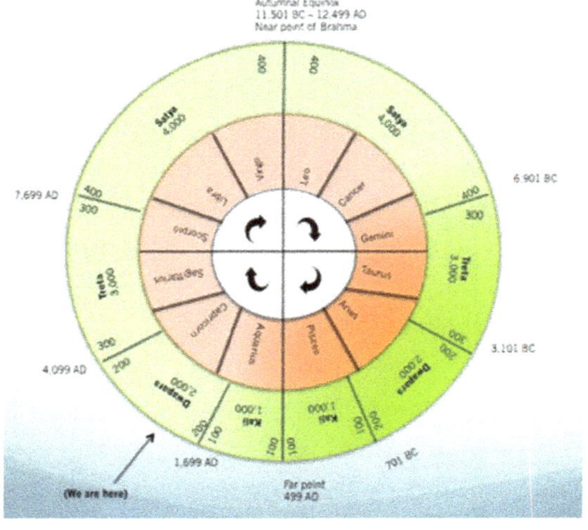

The cycle is divided into two halves – one half is descending when the sun and the solar system move further and further away from its galactic centre to its most southerly point and the other half climbs gradually back to the twelve o'clock high of Satya Yuga.

The period nearest the galactic centre is described in many ancient religions as a golden age of 4,000 years called Satya Yuga, when humanity had direct contact with God and the devatas, and lived in a state of paradise, where war, illness, crime or famine didn't exist and lives were very long and fulfilling.

It is interesting to observe that the greatest and most beneficial times to live in both yugas are side by side and last almost 10,000 years. The same is true for life in the two least desirable periods of the Kali Yuga, which last over 2,000 years.

In modern times, although we have climbed out of those least desirable times, the problems caused when people's mental ability was lowest are all around us, coupled with the habitual patterns of life that went with them. At the moment we are in a time of transmission, where we could jump-start people's mental ability back to 100% or continue the long climb back to 7699 AD with all of its perils and pitfalls...

This has been apparent since the end of the 19th century, when a series of enlightened individuals from India, beginning with the disciples of Rama Krishna, followed by great sages like Yogananda, Maharishi, Karunamayi and Anastasia from Siberia.

My own Guru, Maharishi Mahesh Yogi, has done a great deal to revive the 40 disciplines of the ancient Vedic sciences and Anastasia has filled in the great blank about its history, particularly in Russia. In India they believe that the Vedic civilisation fell apart not long after the Mahabharat War about 5,000 years ago. Although I refer to the teaching of Maharishi and other Self realised Gurus of the modern era to clarify the hidden meaning of the stories, it is important to know that they still practice the timeless, ancient teaching of the Veda and not the modernised version believed by most Hindus today.

Interestingly, Anastasia said that the Vedic civilisation continued as though nothing had happened on 'one small island of the world, which is now called Russia' until about 800AD, when this small island went to sleep and was replaced by Russian Orthodoxy.' She added that a catastrophe of global proportions was supposed to have taken place some years back in the 1990s but the deadline has now passed. She put it down to the efforts of dachniks, people who live on a self-sustaining piece of land. Also there is no doubt that Maharishi also had a big hand in warding off that disaster with the global yagyas he authorised, plus the positive effect of a great many group TM-Sidhi courses.

It is up to everybody to take stock of their essence and rectify the mistake many years ago that allowed the dark forces to usurp God and take control over people's minds across the entire earth. According to Anastasia it took only six men to conquer the earth, not by military conquest but by usurping God and luring people away from the truth by clever images and robotic inventions.

Whether the so-called 'fairy stories' we are re-examining were doctored and transposed by the priests or whether they were originally codified in order to escape being burned, I cannot answer, but what I can tell you is that they were given to me by the goddess Durga to reveal the wonders of the fourth state of consciousness called the turiya state or transcendental consciousness. It is this that gradually purifies the mind and brings about the state of self – realisation, which Maharishi calls cosmic consciousness. This is the state of self-realisation and is the foundation, of the two further states called god consciousness and unity consciousness.

Without this platform no further development is possible. That is why all the modern religions are limited to belief but lack little or no actual experience.

The internal message or task the goddess Durga sent me was: "Be like an explorer. Show people that you have found a new land – turiya – the fourth state, which Maharishi calls transcendental consciousness. It will not only improve their waking, dreaming and sleeping but introduce them to possibilities way beyond anything they had ever dreamed of. Who is going to live there is not your main concern. Show them in your stories that the new land has always been there just beyond the mind, but has been largely forgotten.

Now is the time to awaken everybody to the knowledge that the fourth state is not only there but also holds the answer to all their problems. Explore the stories and tell them how they were meant to be told originally."

It took me completely by surprise when the first area she turned my attention towards was Russian fairy tales. I was especially surprised as I knew nothing about them at all. At that time I had no idea that Russia was the last place on earth to have had a Vedic civilisation. It wasn't until I learned from the Anastasia books that the last vestige of the Vedic way of life had been erased by the introduction of a new language based upon Greek, which was enforced in the 10th century AD. This stopped families from passing on information about life in Vedic Russia.

Life in Vedic Russia and elsewhere was sublime because everyone was in direct contact with God by working with nature. It was this that was the High Priests' main problem. As time passed during the descending yuga, the intellect of mankind fell too so the six priests eventually managed to convince a few of the people that there was an even better way of connecting with the divine through a mediator. Gradually others followed until it became the norm. If we look at all the organised religions on earth, we can see how successful these usurpers were. Whilst all religions convey their version of the truth differently, they are all based upon a mediator acting between a god and 'his' children.

Anastasia said that the self-appointed priests were first successful in ancient Egypt. Thus it is quite likely that there is where the ancient mystery religions began, especially as that is where the *Hermetica* originated. The word 'mystery' has a different connotation in the modern world of today. We associate it with solving some intricate criminal problem in the outside world – many popular novels are of this genre. In ancient times it was linked with the word *mystae*, which means seeing with closed eyes. In other words the initiates had to learn some secret form of meditation that would give them the experience of the fourth state of consciousness called the turiya state, which would bring them into contact with the divine self within, and also purify first their mind, then their emotions, and finally bring unity with God.

However, I didn't shirk the task and began to read the stories. Having had the privilege of receiving an image about their meaning way back in the 1970s, plus gentle revelations from the goddess, I have finally finished a book of standard Russian tales. I thought it best not to change them but leave them the way they are enjoyed at the moment, while also revealing the original hidden intention of the composer in italics wherever necessary to widen the reader's knowledge and enjoyment.

The time is right to redress the mistake by reconnecting with our inner divine self in an easy and natural way. In actual fact, the aim of modern life today is just as it was for the ancient rishis, namely to entertain three main desires – to attain the goal of self-realisation called moksha; to have sufficient wealth and belongings to attain it; and to become free from all other binding desires.

This is the only way of ensuring that the story of all of our lives will be to live happily ever afterwards.

Forest Schools and Mystery Religions

It is my view that the mystery religions and forest schools were synonymous terms for the same Vedic civilisation because they both took place at the same time and had exactly the same aims, namely – that each individual should seek their own spiritual salvation, rather than doing so through a mediator at a church, temple or mosque. The dictionary definition of the word 'mystery' is still to 'reveal the religious truth, which is beyond normal human comprehension', but the popular, modern usage of the word is to describe some earth-bound, gripping suspense play, book or film set somewhere in the exterior world.

We have already established that the ancient meaning of the word *mystae,* meaning seeing with closed eyes. In other words each initiate was guided by a range of suitable techniques from their teacher/guru that would enable their individual mind to dive deeply so as to merge with the underlying turiya state of transcendental consciousness, which would both purify and awaken each person to their inner reality.

Both versions of the name had a very wide church. Everybody was welcome – so there was room for both an exoteric celebration for the many and another for the seekers who were more spiritually advanced.

They followed an oral tradition and used a coded form of storytelling that was easily remembered, which both passed on knowledge and existed as an outline of their whole spiritual journey. They still exist today in what are normally called folktales or fairy stories. Originally they were categorised as myths. The word comes from the Greek *mythos*, – meaning – 'word', 'tale' or 'true narrative', whose facts are rooted in truth. It was only about 400 years ago that scientists and philosophers reclassified them as fictitious tales of superstition or fantasy.

Had they known that there is a larger 12,000 year cycle of time called a yuga which has a bearing on the mental ability of mankind, the same scientists and philosophers would have certainly come to a different conclusion.

It is interesting that Plato said there are four levels of knowledge. These may well correspond to the same four levels of understanding. The top is *mythos* – namely truth, understanding and excellence – because at this level humankind would be in constant contact with the gods who administer the universe in the light of God's plan

The next one down was *dianoia*, which is concerned with teaching people how to think effectively. It was at this level that religion became necessary so as to re-align with the truth.

After this came *pistis,* or faith. This is more or less where we are today, where thoughts and opinions are shaped in us by imitation. They either feel right or we adopt the ethos and values of the society in which we live. This corresponds to the level of understanding resulting from social conditioning.

Finally, Plato sees the fourth and grossest level of understanding as *eikasia,* which represents a total absorption of the images and actions that take place in the exterior world.

However, these dates are not set in stone. Even in the darkest times of the Kali age there are still a number of enlightened gurus who purposely live outside the boundaries of so-called civilised life, so as to interact with the gods who administer the universe. Thus the possibility is always open for any individual to progress spiritually. This and a few well-known aspects of natural phenomena enabled Maharishi Mahesh Yogi to set forth and transform the world to a state of Sat Yuga, even during the darkness of the Dwarpara Yuga.

Maharishi was encouraged to continue studying Physics at university before becoming a devotee of his chosen Guru His Holiness Brahmananda Saraswati. Thus he was able to decipher the ancient knowledge he learned from his Master and explain it clearly in terms of modern Physics. As a case in point....

Just as it only takes 1% of the molecules of ice to change to water to melt the other 99% or to change water into steam, the same is also true of world consciousness – it only takes 1% of the world's population to become enlightened to reinstate the state of Sat Yuga. Unfortunately 1% of 7.6 billion is a colossal number of people – too big to even consider possible – so it was necessary for Maharishi to increase the potency of his system of transcendental meditation by adding the TM-Sidhi programme, which included teaching yogic flying to the most advanced members of his followers. If sufficient numbers of these followers all practised together at the same time it would reduce the number of people needed to become enlightened to only the square root of 1%. Thus, in Russia, with a population of about 144,000,000, this would need only 1200 yogic flyers. In Great Britain, with a population of about 64 million, this would work out to only 800. There is a further proviso – namely to have them situated in the exact centre and holiest part of the country, called the brahmasthan.

However, Maharishi went for gold – he didn't consider individual countries, his target was the whole world. The centre of the world is in India. Therefore this was the best place to send the most positive energy to the rest of the world. The last thing he did before leaving his body was to set up a trust to make this a reality. He estimated that it would take about 8,720 yogic flyers – so, knowing him, he would aim for 10,000 yogic flyers there to achieve a peaceful world.

In the West we are in the habit of equating the mystery religions with the Eleusinian and Orphic models of ancient Greece, but the sage Aurobindo tells us that the Greek mystery schools were a late flowering of what had been taking place for a considerable time before it flowered in ancient Greece. Namely, the folk tales of the mystery religions follow in the same tradition as the Rig Veda – they used the outward trappings of everyday life to tell one aspect of the story, whilst employing the same terms as symbols of a deeply hidden spiritual quest.

The Grimm brothers' version of Cinderella is a good example of this. Even the title throws a light on what the story is really about. Just as the two syllables of the word guru mean darkness and light, the two aspects of the name, 'cinder' and 'ella', mean the same . Ella is a shortened version of Ellen and Eleanor, both of which mean 'light',– so Cinderella is essentially a story about the process of transforming the life of a person trapped in the dark machinations of their own ego into the light of spiritual unity. I will provide a synopsis of this tale in the section 'The Stories'.

Up to the time of the takeover by militants, people were engaged in farming, cultivating the land. A wide network of 'forest schools' existed throughout the land that is now modern Russia and the Ukraine.

Each settlement of individual family domains had their own forest school. Most had a resident teacher, but the villagers also gained a wealth of experience from visiting teachers, who came to give instruction for anything from a few days to a fortnight.

We hear more about male teachers but there is no reason to suppose that there were also many female teachers also. Each one had their own particular areas of expertise in such subjects as cultural customs or art forms. There area of expertise could be poetry, composing songs, traditional dances, knowledge of the stars, the recognition of herbs (where they grew and their medical uses, their perfume and particular essence when added to a certain dish) and a host of others.

These teachers knew how to take their cues from the emotional feeling each individual group gave him and never resorted to the dry intellectualism of today. Knowledge is actually a gift of love which comes about spontaneously from the degree of mutual integration of the teacher and the group consciousness of his or her students.

In the forest school there were different kinds of teachers. But the main teacher was always God represented by the divine teacher, such as Assyris, the son of Svarog. They gave lessons of meditation by explaining, showing, submerging students into His Depth. It was communication with the Teacher and Friend, with the loving Father.

Their teachers explained the essence of the structure of the Absolute and the methods of self-development. Enlightenment is not gained by praying in temples but by meditation and direct interaction with God's creation. These were the two main principles of transforming an ordinary person into God.

Many of the teachers were home-grown but there were others who had attained perfection in other countries, because prior to the Mahabharat War the Vedic civilisation was worldwide.

In addition to the spiritual practices still used by modern gurus they taught circle dances that all people enjoyed, based upon the phenomena of the natural world such as the rhythmic flow of freshwater brooks in the springtime and, the flames of fires. All these were based upon easily observed natural phenomena, which have their own senses of rhythm and dance, such as shining symbols of the Divine Flame!

All of the teachers, such as Assyris, were enlightened. They had attained a very high state of consciousness and were always a great source of divine inspiration to their followers.

One of their main celebrations was at sunrise on the first day of spring. All of the villagers would be there, waiting calmly and quietly. As the sun slowly rose above the horizon they would throw up their arms in joy to greet it. They knew that their body was a replica of the universe, so they looked forward to the new season, whose harvest would be a further deepening of their own consciousness, as well as their own farming domain.

All the teachers gave lessons in meditation. Rather like the seekers of today, who live in the vicinity of their guru, they advanced just by being in his presence. In fact they learned how to immerse themselves in the depth of his consciousness.

It was a blessing that the Kievan Rus managed to continue for another 5,000 years after the final breakup of the Vedic civilisation in other parts of the world.

The decline of the average intelligence of mankind must have resulted in many people having a very literal and fundamental attitude to life, which led to the removal of the last remnants of the Eleusinian mystery temples in the Roman Empire by 395AD. A similar fate occurred in Russia some hundreds of years later. There are two dates for this – both have their own relevance. The history books say it happened when Vladimir the Great, the ruler of Russia, Belarus and the Ukraine (originally called the Kievan Rus) converted to Christianity in 988AD. The other date was calculated by the Siberian sage Anastasia, who said it took place in 800AD. There are two reasons to opt for the latter. Firstly, we can tell that the Sanskrit names of the Rus's gods, such as Perun, were no longer written in Sanskrit, the official language of the forest schools. Secondly, during the Vedic times there was no need for warrior kings or rulers.

Prior to his conversion, Vladimir had been a keen follower of the so-called 'pagan' religious way of life and had erected many shrines to the Slavic gods. As is often the case with people of a fundamentalist disposition, once he had converted, his previous love became a hate. He tore down all the shrines of the old religion he had erected and had the statue of the main Slavic god Perun, dragged through the mud and thrown into the river Dnieper.

This was not all. He and his supporters systematically wiped away the entire history of the Russian nation prior to the conversion, by introducing a new language based on Greek, which made it difficult to pass on the wisdom and customs of the forest schools. The only vestiges of the Vedic past that remain are the Sanskrit names of places, rivers and mountains.

The good news is that the Slavic nations are fortunate to have a modern Siberian sage called Anastasia, whose wisdom is encouraging a revival of the old ways. She is inspiring her ever-growing following to become one with God by interacting with his creation on their own piece of land, called a domain. As she has predicted, as Russia was the last to leave the Vedic culture, it will also be the first one to return to it. It is widely believed that India stopped being a Vedic nation at the onset of the Mahabharat war.

THE ANATOMY OF A' FOLKTALE

Living souls are prisonersof
the joys and woes of existence
To liberate them from nature's magic
the knowledge of the brahman is necessary.
It is hard to acquire, this knowledge,
but it is the only boat to carry one over the
river of Samsara
A thousand are the
paths that lead there.Yet it is one,
in truth,knowledge, the supreme refuge!

- Yoga Upanishad

Mother has died and father has remarried

In many stories such as Cinderella the story opens with the heroine or hero having a very hard time because their mother has died and their father has remarried. Both the stepmother and her two children treat Cinderella as a slave. We will remember that in the *Mahabharat* this happened when King Shantanu went against the conditions that Ganga had laid down prior to their marriage. Consequently he lost her and married Satyavati, leading to the first stirrings of relative creation.

The mother is the source of creation - the absolute - and not a mother as part of a family on earth. Thus she cannot die but she can easily lost to our human awareness because she has all too often been replaced by the stepmother - the ever changing field of relativity. Her two demanding daughters are the mind and senses, both the products of relative creation.

First of all we must remember that each tale is the blueprint of our own journey to enlightenment, so it follows that all the characters in the story are a part of our own psyche. 'Yogananda, reminds us in his book 'god Speaks to Arjuna'

The orphaned child is the buddhi – the heroine. She is the spiritualised intellect, whilst the father is the ego – sometimes positive, negative or indifferent. The buddhi is always the younger child (younger in time) in other words, they were around at the birth of creation and through many lifetimes – not necessarily around for fewer years of life on earth. Her nature is always kind, generous, thoughtful and helpful – thus definitely at odds with the ways of the world in relative life.

Change of Fortune

Every tale has a moment of opportunity to change things for the better. Or to put it more succinctly, to become reconnected with Mother, the source. In the *Mahabharat* it was early in Arjuna's discussion with Krishna that he told him that the way to avoid sin and act in accordance with dharma is to go beyond the three gunas of relative existence into the turiya state – the field of transcendental consciousness.

In the case of the folktale Cinderella it was her father bringing her a sprig from the tree of eternal wisdom, the hazel tree – in other words making a connection with the turiya state, the source. In Jack it was the five magic beans that refined his five senses and made them one with the heavenly world within. In Russian folktales such as the Frog Princess and the Humpbacked Pony, it was reconnecting the mind and buddhi of the hero with the inner guide.

Dismantling the Hut to construct the Palace

This lovely phrase was one used by Maharishi in the early days to new meditators. It is also an apt description for the fairy tale hero or heroine setting off on their journey to enlightenment.

This normally happens by contact, technique or mantra from a recognised guru master who has already completed the journey. The hero/heroine both completes the karma they have brought with them, through the infusion of the turiya – fourth state of consciousness – which also refines their mind and physiology and makes them divine. Thus they often begin life in a rough and ready way, having been born in a hut with very humble origins, and finish the tale by being welcomed into a palace.

In order to help them achieve this they either they follow the advice of their inner guide as in Slavic folklore or they receive help from other forms of natural life such as birds, animals and insects, who are actually messengers of the gods.

The Three Tasks

Thus there are always three standout features of each tale. In Cinderella they were the three appearances at the ball; in Jack and the Beanstalk it was the three visits to the giant's castle. In this book we will use Maharishi's terms for these three higher states of consciousness, namely cosmic consciousness, God Consciousness and Unity Consciousness.

The transition from one state to another comes about by the effusion of pure transcendental consciousness – the basic constituent of life from the underlying turiya state through meditation and Vedic recitation. This not only improves the efficiency and function of the brain and nervous system but also transforms its functioning. Even more interesting, these improvements go far beyond the reach of modern science – they make links with the universe as a whole. Since very ancient times sages have known that the human body is a replica of the cosmic body, summarised through the catchy observation 'as above so below'.

Although the folktales seem to suggest these events take place on consecutive days – they actually can be measured in multiples of twelve years as the human nervous system has to undergo many subtle changes to make each new evolution of consciousness permanent. The change from increasing the awareness of being a separate individual to that of the cosmos itself takes the longest. From then on the two further perfections are said to be more rapid.

Cosmic consciousness

This ties in very well with what Maharishi calls the 'Monarch of the Universe' – a great being who is the sum total of all the star systems and galaxies in the universe. Being very refined, he is described as being able to maintain the excellent order of the universe on a mental level by thought alone. We as individuals have a latent relationship with the cosmic monarch, in just the same way as the cells in our own body have an existence of their own as well as being a component part of something infinitely larger.

Our problem is that we regard ourselves as separate. It is the infusion of transcendental pure consciousness – turiya, the supreme consciousness – underlying our waking, dreaming and deep sleep states during meditation that provides the means whereby we can refine our own nervous system to a degree where it becomes sufficiently fine-tuned to be at one with the cosmic universe.

This was the first of the big initiations in the ancient mystery religions and is called nirvikalpa samadhi in Indian traditions but is better known as cosmic consciousness in the West. Maharishi calls it the merging of the drop back into the ocean and also of an individual's awakening to the Atman – the source of total knowledgeand the inner guide within us all.

He describes it as the full development of the mind. A person achieving this degree of perfection in India is called a swami and can be regarded as a guru, or a knower of reality.

God Consciousness

Maharishi always maintained that true devotion to one or more of the devatas is not possible until one is in cosmic consciousness. The next leg of the journey is from cosmic consciousness to God Consciousness. Whereas cosmic consciousness brings about the full development of the mind, the path to God Consciousness is concerned with the refinement of the senses through devotion to one of the gods. In my own case, whilst I also remain dear to the goddess Durga, she also begins to introduce others.

This is truly the path of love. All the trappings of self-importance vanish. The joy of being close to the inner loved one is all that matters – just being near to her always is both the greatest honour and reward. Whereas one always put one's self first in the past – the position is now reversed. One becomes the dutiful but ever loving servant. One still has one's own ideas and preferences but they are often overruled by the aspect of the deity to whom one is devoted. One always chooses what they wish because they always know best.

Not only does this part of the path bring an individual's organs of action in accord with the will of the gods, it also gradually removes a gap that has developed between the mind; and the hidden reality within. the hidden reality within. Their mind is now at one with the source and their actions in the gross physical universe.

According to traditional Hinduism, there are five dualistic attitudes for approaching God. They describe the nature of the relationship between the devotee and God. They are:

1. Shanta bhava, the peace and stillness felt in the presence of God
2. Dasya bhava, the attitude of a servant towards his Master
3. Sakhya bhava, the attitude of a friend towards a Friend
4. Vatsalya bhava, the attitude of a parent towards a Child
5. Madhura bhava, the attitude of a lover towards the Beloved.

In my own case they are not at all exclusive. My own is mainly the attitude of a servant to his master but there is considerably more warmth than that, so the attitude of a lover to his beloved is also applies. As long as I am considered as the child and my goddess the parent. Vatsalya also applies. Finally, the peace and stillness felt in the presence of God is also there every time I do my TM or enjoy a blissful state of rest in the evening. In fact the more I think about it, there is not really one I could leave out, for all five elements present themselves at the appropriate time.

The sixth state is referred to as God Consciousness, because the individual is capable of perceiving and appreciating the full range and mechanics of creation and experiences, and feeling waves of love and devotion for the creation and its creator. Thus, in this state one not only experiences inner peace, but profoundly loving and peaceful relationships are cultivated with all others.

The sixth state can be defined as the unbounded awareness of Cosmic Consciousness coexisting with the development of refined sensory perception during the three relative states of waking, dreaming, and sleeping. Perception and feeling reach their most sublime level. The finer and more glorious levels of creation are appreciated and every impulse of thought and action is enriching to life.

Unity Consciousness

The seventh and highest state of consciousness is what Maharishi calls unity consciousness. He said that progress towards unity is inevitable once one has reached cosmic consciousness because there are no obstacles or stresses to hold you back. In this exalted state, one experiences being as the basis of everything and permeates every aspect of life. Everything is perceived as the expression of being, even though the diversity of life is still appreciated, one does it in terms of the self.

Only in Unity Consciousness is the gap between inner and outer reality, between subjective and objective existence, completely bridged.

According to Maharishi the transition from God Consciousness to Unity Consciousness is automatic. As devotion intensifies one naturally slips into it. Thus in the most well-known of all folktales – Cinderella – the prince comes for her, signifying that no further effort is needed to achieve unity or marriage with the Divine.

Hazrat Abul Hasan Khirqani summed this up very succinctly: "There are three final states in spirituality. In the first, you consider yourself just as God considers you. In the second state, you become His and He becomes yours. In the third state, you cease to exist and He alone fills thee."

It was the common practice in Vedic times to encode teachings into a symbolic form in stories. In the more familiar myths the hero is one of the gods. Thus Heracles purified his entire mind, body and soul in the process of completing his twelve labours. In folk stories the hero is 'everyman' or 'everywoman' because the obstacles on his or her journey to enlightenment are common to us all. So each story takes the form of an outer journey, which symbolises an inner transformation. Part of this process of transformation – or re-awakening – is to allow the individual to become aware and tease out their real meaning of the tales he had learned by heart.

I would like to go more fully into this symbolism and have chosen the Grimm brothers' version of Cinderella is a good example of this.

The story says the only place Cinderella had for herself was in the hearth. Whilst modern versions of the story have taken this literally and write that the poor girl had to sleep in the fireplace, an initiate would know that she practised a system of bodily and mental purification and spiritual awakening through the internal, spiritual heat of tapasya.

In addition, all the characters in the story are aspects of the same person. Thus the father who initiates the quest is the desire of the ever-restless ego and intellect; Cinderella is the buddhi, that part of the intellect which is open and awake to spiritual growth; and her two ugly sisters represent the increasingly gross aspects of the surface mind and senses.

Early in the story we learn that Cinderella's mother has died and her father has remarried to her stepmother, who is very cruel to her This sounds quite straightforward and normal at a literal level of the mind but at a deeper level an initiate would interpret it entirely differently, namely: on taking birth, all memory of the cosmic mother of us all is still there but beyond recall; and Father, the ego-mind, has become fixated to the ever-changing sphere of relative existence, namely the stepmother, the ever-changing nature of life in the relative universe in which we live.

Similarly, the two ugly sisters are actually the mind and senses, which are constantly involved with the material world, so the buddhi or spiritually awake part of the intellect in the background is generally overlooked.

Father, the ego-driven mind, is always open to fulfil the desires of his three children. In the story, one daughter, the surface mind, wants some clothes that will make her attractive. Another, at a deeper level of the mind, also wants to look attractive but she wants to wear something that will both make her look attractive but also keep its value, so she asks for jewels.

Cinderella, like Ivan in Russian tales, is not worldly wise, so she asks for a sprig of the first branch that knocks against her father's hat. This sounds a bit obscure in modern times but in times gone by it was there was a tradition that men of distinction wore hats and tipping one's hat slightly was a polite form of greeting. Also, there existed a popular saying 'I'll take my hat off to you', referring to someone whose actions and knowledge were more far-reaching and superior to one's own.

Continuing with the story of Cinderella – all her three wishes were fulfilled. The gross, surface mind received her wish for clothes; a deeper aspect was pleased with the jewels; while Cinderella – the buddhi – was given a branch of a hazel tree symbolising eternal wisdom and involving a meditation technique, puja to a deity or japa (or perhaps all three) to practise regularly and thus open her awareness to the purifying, turiya state of transcendental consciousness beyond the waking, dreaming and deep sleep states of consciousness.

Cinderella planted the revivifying sprig of the tree of wisdom on her mother's grave – namely her memory – and watered it three times each day. In other words, she silently repeated the mantra at dawn, midday and dusk and it grew slowly into the tree of wisdom. In Slavic nations this would be symbolised by either the birch or lime.

The story says 'she watered it with her tears'. Nowadays, we always tend to associate tears with sadness but there is another way, far removed from the state of misery, which is called devotion. Maharishi defines this as the 'the result of the cognition of God... that intensified state of love, which unites in a very intimate manner the devotee and his God.' Certainly, some tears may flow but their source has nothing to do with sadness.'

A significant part of the story is that a little white bird comes to perch on the tree and fulfils all of her desires. The fully grown tree is the mind completely refined and purified, which coincides with the state of Cosmic Consciousness, when the individual's awareness is at one with the divine inner reality of the atman. The little white bird represents the active inner deity called the ista devata.

Finally the three trips to the ball correspond to the three initiations into higher states of consciousness. In the story they are said to take place on three consecutive days but in actual fact there would be quite a gap between each one. The first would be the realisation of the divine inner self within. The second is the path of God Consciousness when the atman takes the form of one of the major gods or goddesses to guide one's journey through life. It is a path that facilitates the gradual merging of the two aspects of the self. The third and final is when they finally become one in Unity Consciousness.

Cosmic Consciousness – signifies this as the purification of the mind. Maharishi defines this as: 'the growth of the nervous system'. By growth he means a complete transformation caused by regular purification of the nervous system. 'Due to these modifications brought about by numerous experiences of the turiya state of Transcendental Consciousness it finally becomes permanent.'

The second initiation is the state of God Consciousness, which Maharishi calls the 'reality of the top level of creation'. This path is concerned with the purification of the heart through love and devotion. Maharishi said: 'In order to love someone very great, one has to have a big heart. A small heart just can't swell in waves of love for someone very big. God is not a matter of faith!'

Finally, the third initiation is Unity Consciousness. Maharishi defines this as 'the supreme state of human experience, when one perceives everything in terms of the oneness of the self. In Cosmic Consciousness one lives in harmony with natural law, by gaining support of nature's cosmic creativity. Whereas in Unity Consciousness, one experiences everything as a mode of the functioning of one's own intelligence and gains command over all the laws of nature. The fully developed state of Unity Consciousness is called Brahman Consciousness – the totality of life.'

It is only by achieving these three higher states of consciousness that one can 'live happily ever afterwards'.

In other words, our own journey is very much like Ivan in the stories – because we are so bound up in our own story, our ego gives us the impression that we planned the whole thing, which is far from true. If we look back truthfully and dispassionately at all the significant turning points of our life, we will see that these experiences happened at just the right time in our life spontaneously, without any planning, just as they do for Ivan or the main character in one of the stories. To all intents and purposes it is as if we came into the world again, with our own story already having been written around the bag of unfulfilled desires we have brought with us.

Perun and Indra

The main figure in the Slavic pantheon is Perun, who is the bringer of lightning, thunder and rain. It seems to have been overlooked that his role is exactly the same as Indra's in India.

Indra in India was the most hymned King of the gods in the ancient texts of the Rig Veda, which was highly venerated in ancient times when the Vedic civilisation was predominant. Therefore as both India and all the other countries shared a similar culture it is pretty clear that Indra and Perun were one and the same.

In addition both names seem to have suffered a similar fate – namely that they have been grossly misunderstood in the post-Vedic period, inasmuch as they are both billed as having many human failings. This cannot be true – the leader of the gods, intent on bringing enlightenment and the luxuries of heaven to the earth, cannot suffer from a range of hedonistic desires. The truth of the matter is that Indra has a double role. He is not only the king of the gods but he is also our own inner warrior; a fact which has been pointed out by Aurobindo and Maharishi, my own guru.

To take Aurobindo first: 'In the Veda we have this image of the human soul and the divine riding in one chariot through a great battle to the goal of a high-aspiring effort.'

The chariot is of course the human body, which is a miniature copy of the cosmic purusha. Who else but the king of the gods could help us to elevate it to achieve perfection!

Once again Aurobindo gives us the answer: the divine is there – Indra, the Master of the World of Light and Immortality, the power of divine knowledge which descends to the aid of the human seeker battling with the sons of falsehood, darkness, imitation and mortality. The battle is with spiritual enemies who bar the way to the higher world of our being; and the goal is that plane of vast being becoming resplendent with the light of the supreme truth and uplifted to the conscious immortality of the perfected soul, of which Indra is the master.'

He elaborates further by saying the inner life of man will grow 'into the likeness of the eternal divine by the increasing illumination of knowledge.'

To sum up, Aurobindo concludes: 'the forces and processes of the physical repeat in a symbolic form, the truths of the supra physical which produced it. The same forces and the same processes that govern the physical worlds also govern our inner life and its development. Thus the rishis adopted the phenomena of the physical world as symbols for the functioning and development of the inner life in the concrete language of sacred poetry because ultimately both came from the same source.'

In simple terms: a cow is a symbol of light, – so cows locked in a cave in a mountain means that impulses from our inner nature are being overshadowed by too many desires in the exterior world. Lightning stands for a sudden flash of inspiration, and the dawn is an opportunity to see things in a new and clearer light.

Similarly, Ramana Maharshi reminds us that the same is also true of the Vedanta: 'the true self that we are seeking to realize is not our human self transcient but the universal self, the self that is present in all beings, in all bodies and in the entire world. It is that self which is the witness of all time and space and transcends our psychology, which consists mainly of the incidentals and peculiarities of our personal circumstances and proclivities in life.'

If there are still some doubts about the real nature of Indra, they can easily be put to rest by looking at another ancient Vedic book praising the different qualities of Lord Shiva. The third chapter is a blessing to Shiva in his role of Indra, our inner spiritual warrior, to prevail in battle and defeat all of the enemies preventing us becoming one with the inner light. One of its verses begins: 'raise your voices in shouts of victory for Indra who causes the rains of the fulfillment of all desires.'

Whilst on this particular subject, it is time to assess the character of Veles – who he is and why he sometimes alternates from being good to bad or vice versa.

Maharishi helps us to answer that. We are so used to seeing ourselves as separate from the universe, that we also forget we are miniature replicas of the universe ourselves. Just as Indra is the wholeness of the universe, we are on our way to becoming part of that, and so we too have an Indra in the shape of an inner warrior to help us break through the karmic obstructions we have brought with us.

Agni is the first word of the Veda. It is the seed of creation. As is the case with every seed, it contains every aspect of the development of the plant from its first shoot to its fully grown state, together with its purpose.

That wholeness is Indra. He is the representative of the Absolute. He is the first fully grown seed. We are still the developing shoots in relative creation.

Before we become established in Cosmic Consciousness we too are growing to become one with that wholeness.

Maharishi continues: 'Everything comes out of Agni. In The first wholeness coming from the seed of Agni is Indra. And then there is another Indra to help everyone's house grow into a bigger house.

This explains how Indra grows from a small Indra to a big Indra, and then Brahman. And then there is no greater. This is just the expansion of creation in sequence. Everything comes out of Agni.'

Thus in this context, Veles is really little Indra. He is the one whole which takes us from the root of the tree to its uppermost bough.

Thus in many tales, such as Grey Wolf, we can see *the progressive surrender of the lower being to divine activities so that the limited and egoistic consciousness of the mortal awakens to the infinite and immortal state which is its goal.*

The Frog Princess

Once upon a time in a faraway land there was a great Tsar who had three unmarried sons. He thought it was time they thought about getting married and carrying on their line of succession.

"Each of you must go into a field outside the castle grounds and shoot an arrow as far as you can," he proclaimed. "You must marry whoever lives at the place where your arrow lands."

As all of these ancient tales are about gaining enlightenment, we can be sure that every person and situation in the story pertains to the individual seeker. That being so – the Tsar is God within, the palace grounds are the mind and the seeker's body and the field beyond it is relative creation. The arrows are our unfulfilled desires and our debts and gifts from previous lives.

The three sons carried out their father's wishes. The eldest son's arrow landed in the courtyard of a nobleman, where it was picked up by the nobleman's daughter. The middle son's arrow landed in a merchant's yard, where it was found by the merchant's daughter, whilst his youngest son Prince Ivan shot his arrow the furthest. He followed the path it had taken. It led him to a swamp, where he was surprised to see a frog holding an arrow in its mouth. Being a dutiful son, he did what his father had asked, with the result that all three sons were married.

Whilst the outer meaning of marriage is generally taken to be a lifelong commitment to a partner we are all conversant with the term 'married to one's job' or role in life – in other words that role to which the mind gives most thought. This is how it must be taken in this story. Thus the three sons refer to levels of the mind. The eldest son stands for the surface level of the senses – the grossest form of cognition; the second son is the level dealing with surface thoughts down to the intellect; and the youngest represents the buddhi or spiritualised intellect.

Before coming into this world, everybody comes into this world with four objectives: to live in accordance with dharma or their religion; to work through their karma or debits and credits they bring from previous existences; to be able to keep and sustain ourselves and our dependents; and finally and most importantly to attain moksha – or release from the endless cycle of birth and death.

No story of a life can end happily ever after without first attaining this necessary condition. In order to fulfil this prime objective, people must become as familiar with the fourth state – transcendental consciousness – as we are with the states of waking, dreaming and deep sleep. The transcendent is the underlying source and support of everything in creation.

The arrow of the buddhi landed in the mouth of a frog. How can it be that a common frog can be regarded as the source and sustainer of all creation? Easily, if we go back to the great traditions of the distant past such as the Vedic tradition of India and ancient Egypt.

A hymn in the Rig Veda *speaks of a great frog creating and supporting the universe and everything in it. Similarly, the ancient Egyptians had a goddess of childbirth and fertility, called Hecket, who had a female body and a frog's head.*

As frogs are at home in two different mediums, water and land, they represent the two very different fields of the infinite and formless Absolute and that of relative creations, with all of its myriad forms. As one would expect, these concepts became watered down with the passing of time. In the classical cultures of Greece and Rome, the frog still persisted as symbols of Aphrodite and Venus for harmony and fertility amongst lovers.

Today it has all but slipped out of sight – but not quite. In building terms, the indent in the centre of a brick, where most of the mortar is placed, is still called the frog. So even today it is still the term frog which joins with every other brick in our walls and buildings.

As one would expect, this made Prince Ivan the laughing stock of his two elder brothers. This made him very sad, but he kept to his side of the bargain and treated the frog as if she was a princess – at least she was able to speak.

This is very up-to-date. Many people who follow a religious way of life today are scorned as being unworldly and superstitious. What doesn't come over in the story is that Ivan's frog wife is actually his inner guide or hidden advisor. Although she is unseen, everything he does is through her grace and will.

One day the Tsar called his three sons to him.

"I want each of your wives to make me a shirt – the best possible she can make in the time – by tomorrow morning."

The first two sons went off excitedly to tell their wives, whilst Prince Ivan was more subdued.

"Is anything the matter?" asked the frog.

"You could say that!" he retorted. "My father wants you to sew him a beautiful shirt by tomorrow."

"Oh don't let worry you, my prince," she replied. "Just go to bed and forget it. Morning is much wiser than evening."

Obviously a Russian shirt is not the plain, utilitarian garment one puts on without much thought in the West. Just as a breast-plate was used as a protection against swords, arrows and spears in wartime, a shirt was a protection against malignant occult forces that could strike one at any time. As you can see from the pictures they were handmade by crafts-people and decorated with talismans and shields, which served as both a defence and an outward decoration.

The illustration on the left shows that a man's shirt had to have talismans around the collar, the cuffs and the hem at the bottom. In the 18th century the shield featuring sacred symbols of protection first appeared in Siberia and then moved to the European part of Russia. It is most likely that a man would have consulted a competent astrologer or shaman, who would have known the symbols that would give the most protection. The designs were embroidered on a rectangular piece of cloth super-imposed upon the shirt. Women's blouses followed the same patterns as the men and were not tucked in but worn outside the trousers or skirt, often with a belt.

However, the greatest protection one can have is to be invincible so that no hidden occult force can assail one. This state, where a person has made all the necessary links to be permanently at one with the cosmos, is called Cosmic Consciousness. Maharishi Mahesh Yogi said that once a person transcends, he or she experiences bliss consciousness. When one comes back to the activity of relative life some of the bliss remains. Regular infusions of the Transcendental Consciousness cultivate the human nervous system to be sufficiently flexible to remain in bliss consciousness at all times in activity. He said that the mind becomes so intimately familiar with the state of being that it becomes permanently grounded in it.

This is the kind of ultimate protection that the Tsar – as god – would have had in mind for his sons. Maharishi says that this exalted state is humans' birthright, which has become lost in the long lapse of time and should be restored as soon as possible to make life on earth sweet and enjoyable for everyone.

That night when everyone was asleep the frog turned into Vasilisa the Wise. She clapped her hands and said "Come, my

A shirt with talismans, replica. Archangel region.

A "shied" of a young bachelor's shirt, replica. Baykal Lake region.

maids and servants, Sew me a shirt like the one I saw at my dear father's."

In the morning Ivan awoke to find a most elegant and beautiful shirt lying on a chair waiting for him. Without any ado he picked it up joyously and rushed to take it to show his father. The Tsar loved the one that Ivan had brought but didn't care much for the ones his other daughters-in-law had made.

It is easy to forget that whenever a folktale speaks of three brothers or three sisters, these are actually not three people, but three different depths or aspects of the mind. The youngest always comes off best because they symbolised the buddhi or refined, spiritualised intellect. It is also interesting that the frog is actually Vasilisa the Wise, known as Saraswati in India.

A few days later the Tsar set another task.

"I want your wives to bake the finest bread for me by tomorrow," he said to his three sons.

It is well known that many Russian people believe that the world is full of spirits which live next to people but are rarely seen by us. They can be both helpful or malicious but with proper recognition and respect they can make a positive difference to our lives by helping us in times of difficulty.

There are many sayings about bread in many cultures. Bread has a special significance for Slavic tribal people. It is the most sacred food, a gift from God, a living being, and a form of deity itself. Bread is the quintessential offering for Slavic people, as it symbolizes the relationship of exchange between the humans and God, between the living and their ancestors.

We often hear the term half-baked when some task hasn't been completed or thought through properly. This is the case with this particular story. Although Prince Ivan was now in a very high state of consciousness, his spiritual evolution was far from over.

Maharishi has made it clear that cosmic consciousness is the full development of the mind but that is not the end of the story. The next step is to refine the senses so as to be able to experience the realm of the devatas at the finest level of relative existence.

This he calls God Consciousness. This is the sphere of life in which the smooth and efficient order of the earth and the universe is maintained. Thus the ecological problems of our own world only exist because we choose to try and buck these natural laws for humans' own short-sighted financial advantage.

This is the second major step in anybody's spiritual evolution.

When the three sons took the bread their wives had baked to the Tsar, he chose the one baked by the frog princess to be easily the best.

"I have some good news for you," said the Tsar. "Tomorrow we are having a sumptuous feast. I invite both you and your wives to turn up in their finest clothes for the occasion."

Prince Ivan went home and told his wife about the invitation.

"Don't worry yourself about it Ivan," she answered kindly, putting his mind at rest. "You will go on alone but I will arrive a little later."

Next day Prince Ivan made his way to the Tsar's palace on his own. As one would expect, his brothers and their wives made fun of him, saying: "Where's your wife, Ivan? We expect she'll be hopping along later!"

Suddenly they all heard a thunderous sound approaching the palace. They turned round and saw a golden carriage driving up to the entrance. The door of the carriage opened and the most beautiful woman they had ever seen stepped out of the carriage. It was Vasilisa the Wise. Even more astonishingly, she took Prince Ivan by the hand and led him into the feast.

After sitting at the dinner table eating the main course of baked swan, Vasilisa had a few tricks to show them. She put some of the swan bones up one of her sleeves and poured the rest of the wine from her glass up her other sleeve. Her sisters-in-law were entranced by her beauty and followed suit by copying what they had done.

After the meal everyone got up to dance. Whilst Vasilisa was dancing with Ivan she waved the first sleeve, whereupon a huge lake appeared. When she waved the other several pure white swans appeared on it.

Seeing the miracle that Vasilisa had just performed, her two sisters-in-law wanted to show off and be at least her equal, so they both waved their sleeves, but only succeeded in splashing the other guests with wine and throwing a lot of old bones on to the dance floor.

According to Nithyananda, the significance of the swan is to symbolise liberated consciousness.

There are so many allusions to the swan that Vasilisa must be a Russian form of Saraswati, the goddess of knowledge, poetry, the arts and music. The name Saraswati means lake and her vehicle is the swan. The lake is the limitless waters of pure consciousness. The swan floating on the lake whose surface is as smooth as a mirror reflects perfectly the serenity and purity of mind necessary for clear and beautiful language and devotional hymns.

This is what Maharishi said about Saraswati:

'Saraswati has been covered by ignorance, thus the source of all knowledge has been hidden beneath the three alternating states of waking, dreaming and deep sleep. The uncovering of Saraswati brings enlightenment. She is the source of the Veda, which awakens the intellect to the totality of creation.

All thoughts come from the source of thought. When the mind is awake at this level, it is awake to Saraswati. Thoughts not appreciated at their initial level of purity are bound to bring confusion to an individual's mind because they no longer reflect the pure nature of the initial desire.'

Mother needs to be at home in the basis of our awareness. She has three main aspects: Saraswati is the silent unbounded lake of pure consciousness; Mahalakshmi is the total wealth of knowledge awake in the self and Durga is the organising power that brings its evolving march to absolute fruition.

Prince Ivan was so overjoyed for everyone to see that he had such a wonderful wife that he ran home whilst everyone else was still at the feast. He wanted to keep his wife as she was so he ran off to burn her discarded frog skin so that she would remain beautiful for everyone to see.

When she arrived home she was sad because she couldn't find her frog skin.

"Ivan, you have no idea what a silly thing you have just done. If you had waited just a few more days I would have been your wife forever. But now I must depart and go and live as the prisoner of Koschei the Deathless." – With that she changed into a swan and disappeared.

Koschei is the arch demon in many Russian and Polish folktales. In many of them he abducts the heroine. He is very difficult for the hero to kill because he can change his appearance at will. Also his soul is separate from his body so he cannot be killed by conventional means.

Just as Vasilisa the Wise is the Russian version of Saraswati – the goddess of wisdom, the arts and music – so is Koschei similar to Ravana, who abducts Rama's wife Sita in the famous Ramayana*; and also very much like the demon king in the* Devi Mahatmyan*, who is eventually slain by the great goddess Durga. In the latter – which is a famous puja about the destruction of our shadow self, the ego – the goddess succeeds in overcoming his six major manifestations: the complaining faces of too much and too little; anger; passion; and finally self-deprecation and self-conceit. As if this wasn't enough, he is also the seed of all desires: greed, envy, anger, attachment, delusion and arrogance.*

The ego is situated beyond the sphere of our intellect. It is like a phantom that tends to direct all of our attention outwards towards the gross environment. It acts like a person who stands with his back to the sun, thus throwing a shadow in every direction we look. Whilst everything is done in the sphere of the infinite, the ego picks up the thought from its own level of intelligence and acts in accordance with its own experience rather than letting perfection prevail.

It was Ivan's impetuous action of wanting things his own way rather than obeying the correct laws that underlie all of life that meant that the wise goddess was veiled from him.

Ivan was very upset and went searching for his wife. On the way he met an old man, who told him what had happened.

"Vasilisa's father turned her into a frog because she was wiser than he. If you want to find her, Ivan, take this ball and follow it as it rolls along the ground.

I remember Maharishi's three-step march to the goal of life on his 'Perfect Man' course. It was Atman, Vishwa, Brahm. In other words, first the individual has to make contact with his/her inner guide, which in our story Ivan already has; next he becomes one with the universe; and finally become one with Brahman, who is beyond name and form.

Ramana Maharshi's description is similar but on the other side of the coin: 'from the Imperishable comes the Unmanifest or Avyakta. From Avyakta / Unmanifested comes Hiranyagarba, the primordial Egg. From Hiranyagarbha, the whole universe projects.'

Having already purified the mind, the next step is to refine and purify the heart and the senses. Maharishi said that it is not strictly possible to be a bhakti or true devotee until one has reached Comic Consciousness because the next leg of the inner journey is to achieve God Consciousness, sometimes called refined Cosmic Consciousness because this is when the heart is opened to the divine self of all existence. This is what Ivan has now embarked upon.

The old man would be Lord Brahma, the creator of the universe. The ball is the hiranyagarbha, the golden egg of all creation. First of all, it is necessary to have a full picture about creation. Once again we will call upon Ramana Maharshi.

I have followed the line of the story and said that the old man Prince Ivan met was Lord Brahma. However, we must remember that these wisdom tales are very old, thus when they were first conceived the deity may well have been feminine. Take the case of an ancient goddess named Meenakshi, who is still the main target of worship even though it is now a temple to Lord Shiva in Madurai. The first lines of the Meenakshi Stotram *are as follows:*

'Salutations to Meenakshi, who is goddess of Madurai,

Who has a bird in her hand, who is the daughter of the pandya king,

Who is Gauri, who has a temple near a golden lotus tank,
Who is the darling of Lord Sundereswara,
Who is the goddess Uma, who likes to play with the golden ball
In the forest of kadamba trees.'

The same feminine supremacy is also shown in the Lalita Sahasranama. The name number 637, vishva garbha, means 'she has the universe in her womb'. Name 934 says she is vishva mata – 'the mother of the universe and of everything in it'.

Now back to the hiranyagarbha. The quotation for name number 638 is svarna-garbha, which states:

'She has the golden egg in her womb or she was born from a golden egg. A 17th century text called the Vedanta-paribhasha *says that 'Hiranyagarbha is the first soul to be born and is different from Brahma, Vishnu and Shiva.'*

The subtle body consists of five sheathes from the five basic elements of akasha, air, fire, water and earth. There are two kinds of subtle body – the superior subtle body of the hiranyagarbha is called mahat or the cosmic intellect, whilst the inferior subtle body of the individual is called the ego.

From the above, we can see that Prince Ivan has to become one with the cosmic intelligence if he is to be reunited with Vasilisa the Wise.

At the highest level of phenomenal existence, the terms god, Ishwara, Prajna and Aum – the creative word – belong to the category of the unmanifest, becoming the manifest universe of beings and matter.

These are derivatives of the imperishable and immeasurable Brahman. There is no descent, no reduction, and no diminution. As per the Brahma-sutras, Ishvara is Brahman with creative energy. His Maya-sakti is the mediating cause of this phenomenal world. Isvara is both transcendent and immanent. He is transcendent in relation to Brahman and immanent in relation to the created world. This immanence is not a descent from transcendence for the sake of upasana or worship. They are the two sides of the same coin, one side is Brahman and the flipside is

Isvara – no pun is intended. Brahman is maya-free and Isvara is a mayin. Brahman and transcendence have to be without attributes and so are maya-free. Brahman transcends three gunas, which is known as trigunaatita (three gunas transcended).

Prajna is knowledge through intuition and self-realization. Prajna is transcendental wisdom.

Brahman becomes isvara or a personal god with pure wisdom / prajna. Brahman doesn't diminish or cease to be by becoming isvara. Isvara is an adjunct status.

Isvara is the principle behind the mulaprakriti or the unmanifested, the inner guide of all souls. Isvara can take the form best suited to guide each and every individual he guides. Thus the personal Atma is not tied to any particular religion or way of life. He knows the past experiences and capabilities of each individual but leaves it up to the free will of the individual to choose the correct path and practice of refinement.

At Level Two: Isvara is the immediate cause of hiranyagarbha – the embryo of the world. This embryo stage is comparable with the dream state, complete with ideas and possibilities. The embryo stage is an internalized stage. Brahma is the creator of this dream world of possibilities.

The third phenomenal level is that of viraat or manifestation. This is when Hiranyagarbha – the embryo is projected into space and time and we get viraat or manifestations.

Ramanuja says that Isvara is the inner controller of cit and acit – Beings and universe, sentient and insentient. When the embryo stage is thus exteriorized, the manifest world is like the waking state. When retrograde involution takes place, the cit, the acit, hiranyagarbha, and isvara go (trace their steps backwards) into Brahman.

The gospel of John states, like the Veda says, 'in the beginning was the word.' That word is often written as Om. It is the master plan incorporating all the laws of nature and it creates all the different levels of creation. Strictly, taking Sanskrit as the language of the infinite, Om is spelled as AUM. It straddles all levels of existence and is imperishable. A is for the waking state, U is for the dream state and M is for the deep sleep. The silence that follows AUM is the turiya. This is the same as what Maharishi calls the fourth state of transcendental consciousness. Aum is worshipped as Isvara with a form and Brahman as formless.

Ivan saw a bear and followed it into the forest. Feeling very hungry, he was about to shoot the bear with his bow and arrows but was stopped in his tracks by the entreaty of the bear:

"Don't kill me, Prince Ivan," it said. "I will be able to help you in the near future." The prince heeded his advice and journeyed on further into the forest.

It was fortunate that Ivan's hunger for the truth of enlightenment was stronger than his desire for food for the senses. The bear is the emblem of Russia. Symbolically it stands for resurrection and is the alchemical cipher for the primary state of matter, towards which Ivan is heading.

A little further on, Ivan came across a drake. As before, he took out an arrow and put it on his bow ready to shoot but the drake begged him not to:

"Don't kill me, Prince Ivan. I can be very helpful to you later."

Similar to the frog in The Well at the World's End, *who is at home in the two different environments of land and water, the duck is a mediator between water and sky – the sky in this case is the element of space or akasha from which everything is made. It is significant that Ramana Maharshi calls this the stem substance whilst Maharishi calls it the colourless sap, which permeates everything in creation.*

So Ivan kept on walking. The further he went, the hungrier he felt. Soon he came across a rabbit but once again resisted the idea of killing it because it begged him not to and said that it will help him later.

The rabbit or hare is associated with the moon in many ancient cultures. In the context of this story it is one of two extra chakras and is situated between the ajna or third eye and the journey's end, the thousand-petalled lotus at the top of the head of the subtle body. The job of the moon chakra is to turn every-

thing a yogi or devotee eats into soma, thus making his body spiritual.

On the last leg of the journey Ivan encountered a pike by the seashore. It was lying stranded on the beach, gasping to be put back into the water.

"Don't kill me," it gasped. "Put me back into the water. I will be helpful to you later."

Once again Ivan's good nature prevailed. He lifted the great fish, put it back into the sea and continued onwards.

Fish were important symbols in all ancient cultures. When portrayed as swimming downwards they represented the involution of the spirit into matter and when depicted as swimming upwards it was the evolution of the spirit returning to its first principle, as was the case with Ivan.

Now back to the story – Prince Ivan is following the golden ball back to its source in Ishvara. We have to remember that Ishvara can be both the Absolute self without form and also as a god with form because he straddles the line of demarcation between the formless Absolute and the very finest aspect of relative creation.

Soon afterwards, Prince Ivan was following the golden ball back to its source, when he came upon a strange little hut standing on chicken's legs, where Baba Yaga lived.

Baba Yaga is now portrayed as the kind of terrifying figure that would scare most adults to death, let alone their children. She is said to be old, bent and ugly. She lives in a hut which stands upon chickens' legs and can spin of its own accord. She can also fly through the air seated in her mortar and pestle.

Whenever a new religion is gaining ground it people often finds it necessary to demonize the previous one. I am sure that Baba Yaga is a prime example of this. In today's world she is shown as the complete epitome of ugliness and deception but even so it is hard to completely hide the compassion, wisdom and generosity she possesses, characteristics that one would associate with an aspect of Mother Divine. Even after the character assassination she is the held to be the guardian spirit of the fountain of the Waters of Life and of Death and rules over the elements.

The fact that Ivan's next port of call is Baba Yaga shows that she is indeed Ishvara. So the witch that terrifies Russian and Slav people in general is not a witch at all. She is really the mother of us all. In the Vedic tradition, she is the three-in-one – Durga, Mahalakshmi or Saraswati – depending on what role she is playing and also what she is bestowing. It is Lakshmi for wealth of all kinds and Saraswati for knowledge. Durga is both the organising power that distributes gifts from the other devatas and also the remover of obstacles. That is why the three goddesses are always together in a Hindu temple. Being the organiser and distributor, Durga is usually in the centre with the other two great goddesses on either side of her.

Why is her home described so strangely, as having the ability to spin round whilst standing upon chicken legs? That question always being asked gives us the main clue – which came first, the chicken or the egg? Being Ishvara, she laid the golden egg bringing about creation. Her hut is able to spin like a coin because its two sides are facing the formless Absolute and relative creation. She is both transcendental and immanent. Thus she is what Maharishi calls 'all possibilities'.

In this light it is easy to see that her three magic horsemen are not just dawn, noon and midnight. Their colours (red, white and black) are also the colours of the three gunas which make up everything in creation. Without them even Ishvara couldn't create. In addition dawn, noon and midnight are junction points in the day when it is easier to meditate and have access to the pure field of creative intelligence underlying all matter.

Whilst disrobing the hideous faces and appearances the Kali age has dressed her up in, we can ask who the three pairs of hands which carry out all her work are. Modern Hindus would say Brahma, Vishnu and Shiva, but it is really their shaktis Mahalakshmi, Durga and Saraswati that do everything – their husbands are their flipsides, who remain in the Absolute.

How can I be so sure about this? Because the goddess Durga gave me this knowledge as a waking gift on Monday 28 November 2011. On my own I would never have seen through the tangled web of images.

I am not trying to say that the hideous garbs pinned on to Mother Divine are deliberate. It is all down to how much light is available. Most people have been startled in poor light by initially thinking that a pair of rolled-up socks or tights under the wardrobe were a large rat or mouse. The same thing happens in the mental sphere. If our consciousness is murky we are bound to get the wrong impression or viewpoint but once the mind regularly experiences the wonderful washing machine of pure consciousness, we are able to see things more clearly.

There is one more piece of telling evidence that Baba Yaga is actually Mother Divine: her vehicle. At first it sounds quirky to travel about sitting inside a mortar holding a pestle, until we examine the symbolism behind this bizarre image. The mortar is the hollow feminine receptive vessel in which the pestle crushes the elixir of life and immortality.

"What are you doing here?" asked Baba Yaga, knowing that Prince Ivan would be searching for wisdom, knowledge and truth or else he couldn't have arrived there.

"Hey mother!" He chirped the usual incantation: 'First you satisfy my hunger, then you satisfy my thirst, then let me immerse myself in your purifying banya (sauna), then let me sleep in pure consciousness and then you ask me anything."

She smiled as she always did and did as he asked, as she was specifically favourable to heroes or heroines with pure hearts.

"Well – what did you come for?" she asked mischievously, knowing exactly why he had come.

"I have come looking for Vasilisa," Prince Ivan replied. "Can you tell me where I can find her?"

"I certainly can," she winked. "But it's not going to be easy. She is being held as a captive in the palace of Koschei the Deathless. You must understand that Koschei is terribly dangerous. He watches her day and night and it is almost impossible to kill him because his soul is separate from his body. The only way he can be killed is by breaking the magic needle in which his soul is hidden. Koschei treasures that tree and spends as much time watching that tree of life as he spends watching Vasilisa."

Ivan listened carefully to Baba Yaga's instructions.

"The needle is in an egg; the egg is in a duck; the duck is in a rabbit; the rabbit is in a stone chest; and the stone chest is on top of a tall oak tree."

Baba Yaga's cryptic message is telling Ivan to meditate and go deep with himself to the source of creation to find the needle and thus put an end to the machinations of the ego Koschei. Maharishi says that being only aware of the manifest universe is a 'mistake of the intellect, which makes a person unaware of the inner truth within.

The symbolism is as follows- the stone chest is the mind and senses. The rabbit is the moon alias the mind and intellect. In the original story the 'duck' would have almost certainly have been the swan of the goddess Saraswati, the creator of the 'hiranyagarbha'. This Sanskrit word translates as 'the golden embryo, the golden womb or the golden egg' as it is in this story.

"Thank you for all your help, Baba Yaga," smiled Ivan. He waved and went on his way.

The oak tree was one of the two trees representing the relative universe in Slavic folklore. By pulling it up shows that Ivan wants to experience the deeper truth within himself through meditation.

Not long afterwards he saw the massive oak tree standing in front of him. What could be done? It was too tall to climb and too wide and strong to cut down. All of a sudden the bear he had spared appeared and tore up the tree by its roots.

As one can imagine this is no ordinary bear. In Slavic mythology and folklore the bear is often used as a cipher for man- notably as a father, husband or fiancé. Incidentally, the bear is the only animal that walks on two legs. It is the Great Bear we see in the night sky, which we have in miniature form in our own heads. The seven stars which give it its shape are called the seven wise rishis in the Vedic tradition. These are the wise seers who cognised the sounds of the Vedic mantras in their minds at the birth of time. They are the sounds which create everything in the universe.

The tree actually symbolises the attachments and aversions of the ego to everything in relative creation. In the Veda this tree is called Vanaspati and has a multitude of branches in all of the fourteen universes. Once this is demolished in us there can be no more fear due to the duality of the mind and emotions, only eternal contentment and happiness.

Once the huge tree was uprooted, the stone chest fell out and broke. Out jumped the rabbit.

Stone was worshipped widely in ancient cultures on account of its stability, reliability, permanence and indestructibility. As such stones could be seen as immortal. Also, as they could fall as meteorites, they were seen to have a connection with the sky. Even today a black meteoric stone is the centrepiece of ritual worship for Muslims in Mecca. Stone carved and worked upon like the one in this story denotes a person that has been worked upon and perfected.

The rabbit started to run away but the one that Ivan had spared suddenly appeared and intercepted it. A duck flew out from the rabbit and tried to fly away but the drake that Ivan had spared caught it. The egg fell out of the duck and into the sea. However, before it could sink, the pike that Ivan had spared brought to him. He opened the egg and broke off the point of the needle, with the result that Koschei lost his strength and died instantly in his palace.

One may well ask why the needle was so important. To answer that we have to remember what the Vedic scriptures say: 'You are not the body or the mind.' Why is this, when they are so intimate to us and are with us every moment of our waking lives?

Our true nature is really the transcendental absolute pure consciousness. It is the needle of the ego that has stitched all of our past experience, knowledge and aspirations into a cloak that masks our essential self. That is why transcending is so important because it cultivates the mind and nervous system to function in tune with our underlying self. Once the sewing instrument is broken, the inner reality dawns brightly.

It is also significant that the hiranyagarbha represents the dream state of consciousness. It is hard to imagine that this life is really a waking dream but that is the case.

Ivan was now safe to enter Koschei's vast dominion. He found the palace in which his dear wife was a prisoner. Prince Ivan was delighted to see her again and took her home, where they lived happily for the rest of their days.

Marya Morevna

Introduction

Before beginning this story, it is necessary to quote a short version of a hymn given by the rishi Markendaya to a one-time king who is now the manu of the universe. I am quoting Swami Satyananda Saraswati's translation of *Atha pranandikam*, which means 'the most preeminent secret' from his book *The Chandi Path*. The king wanted to know the precise appearances and natures of the great goddess and how each should be worshipped.

Keshavadas tells us that the great goddess has six main manifestations, namely: Prakriti, Durga, Lakshmi, Saraswati, Gayatri and Radha. She is the creative power known as prakriti – *pra* means origin and *kriti* means creation. The swami's translation is as follows:

'The supreme Sovereign – the great goddess of true wealth , who is comprised of the three qualities, is the first and foremost of all causes. Her intrinsic nature is both definable and indefinable and having distinguishes all the individual phenomena of the universe, She resides within.

Oh King, She holds a pomegranate (symbolising the unity of creation), the, club, the shield and drinking vessel, and on her uppermost part She bears a snake which unites the male principle) with the female principle of energy.

Her beauty is comparable to melted gold, and her ornaments shine like melted gold.. She filled the entire nothingness with Her radiant light.

Seeing the entire Nothingness, the Supreme Sovereign assumed another form the quality of darkness.

That form became a beautiful woman whose radiant body was as black as soot. Her finely shaped mouth has large protruding teeth. Her eyes were large and waist thin.

In Her four hands She displayed the sword, the drinking cup, a severed head, and shield, with decapitated bodies forming a necklace, and a garland of skulls worn over her head.

Having thus appeared, that manifestation of Darkness, excellent among women, said to the Great Goddess of True Wealth: "Mother, again and again I bow down to you. Give to me my names and describe the duties I have to perform."

Then the Great Goddess of True Wealth said to the Excellent Lady of Darkness, "I give to you your names and the various actions which you will perform.

The Supreme Sovereign replied:

You will be known as The Great Measurer of Consciousness, the Great Remover of Darkness; the Great Destroyer of Hunger and Thirst; Sleep and Desire. Solely attentive to Battle against the Dark Night, the Impassable.

These are your names indicative of the actions which you will perform. One who knows your activities by meditating upon these names attains the highest happiness."

Oh King, thus having spoken, the Great Goddess of True Wealth assumed another divine female form, possessing the lustre of the moon by means of the pure quality of Light, assumed another form with radiant lustre like the moon.

This supreme woman held in her hands the rosary of alphabets, the curved sword, the lute or vina, and a book and She too was given names.

The Great Knowledge, the Great Vibration, the Light of Wisdom, sound, the Spirit of All-Pervading Knowledge, She who Purifies with Wisdom, Creative Energy, the Cow who Fulfils all Desires, the Womb of Wisdom and Lord of the Mind.

Then the Great Goddess of True Wealth said to the Great Remover of Darkness and the Spirit of All-Pervading Knowledge:"Goddesses, you both produce pairs , male and female, according to your natures".

Thus having instructed them, the Great Goddess of True Wealth first produced Her own pair: a male and a female of beautiful appearance, seated upon a lotus seat, having come from the Golden Womb, (the first spark of creation also known as bindu)_.

Then the Mother, the Great Goddess of True Wealth, said to the male, "Knower of Consciousness, Systematic Worship, the Shining One, Creator."

And again to the female, " Ultimate Prosperity, Lotus Blossom, Goddess of Wealth, and in this way gave their names"

The Great Remover of Darkness and the Light of Wisdom also produced pairs according to their natures. I am telling you their names.

The Great Goddess of Darkness gave birth to a male who had a blue throat, red arms, a white body and also wore a digit of the moon on his forehead, as well as a white female.

He is known as: the Reliever of Suffering, the Cause of Peace, the Permanent Resident, of Matted Hair, with Three Eyes; while the female is called the true, Knowledge, the Cow Fulfilling All Desires, Language, Letters and Melody.

Oh King, the Spirit of All-Pervading Knowledge brought forth a female of bright colour and a male who was dark. I am telling you their names.

The names: Consciousness Which Pervades All, the Doer of All, Ruler of the Senses, the God of True Wealth and the Lord of Existence apply to the male;and the Nourishing Mother, She Who is Rays of Light, the Energy Which Tears Thought Apart, the Beautiful, Excellent Fortune and the Energy of Infinite Goodness apply to the female.

In this way the three young ladies took the form of males. This fact those who see with the eye of wisdom will understand but other uninitiated people may not understand the esoteric meaning of this secret.

Oh King, the Great Goddess of True Wealth gave the Spirit of All Pervading Knowledge to the Creative Capacity As a wife, and to the Reliever of Suffering, She gave She Who is Rays of Light, and to the Lord of True Wealth she gave the Ultimate Prosperity .

Thus the Creative Capacity and his Wife, the Spirit of All pervading Knowledge, gave birth to the Cosmic Egg; and the Reliever of Suffering, along with his wife, She Who is Rays of Light, pierced the egg and caused it to crack.

Oh King, within the egg were all the primary products, the capacity of the five elements to unite, and all this existence of moveable and immovable forms came to be.

Then the Great Goddess of True Wealth, along with the Consciousness which Pervades All, began to protect and to nourish creation, and at the appointed time, the Great Lord with His wife, She Who is Rays of Light, will cause its dissolution.

Oh Great King, the Great Goddess of True Wealth is the Ruler of All Truth and of the quality of Light. She is the inconceivable formless, and again She is with form and is known by many names.

Only her attributes can be names, and yet She cannot be explained by only one name.

Marya Morevna

A long time ago in a Russian kingdom closer than you might think lived a Tsar and his Queen, with their son Ivan and three daughters Maria, Olga, and Anna.

These three characters – in a story book form – symbolise the first three sequential steps, prior to creation and the birth of everything in the universe. The Tsar is Brahman, who is beyond name, form and gender. The Tsarina is Mother Divine, who is the source of everything in creation. She in turn produces from herself the three mothers, exactly reflecting the first part of Satyananda Saraswati's translation of the hymn.

The kingdom or state in question is the fourth state of consciousness, which transcends the waking, dreaming and deep sleep states called turiya or transcendental consciousness. As the story says, this kingdom is much closer to us than we think. So close in fact that we would have no life without it. It is the deepest part of our being and is available between each breath we breathe and each thought we think. It only becomes obvious to us when we transcend the finest thought of the restless mind during meditation and enter the stillness and serenity of the turiya state of consciousness.

As regards its size, the holy book of the Veda *says that although the universe with all its stars, suns and planets is said by scientists to be infinitely large, it is still only one quarter of the size of the vast kingdom or sphere of existence that gives rise to it, supports it and then takes it back into itself.*

The years passed and it was time for the old Tsar to hand over his kingdom to his son on his deathbed. On his deathbed the Tsar instructed young Ivan to see that his sisters Maria, Olga and Hannah were properly married and taken care of while they were still fresh and young.

The meaning of their names is interesting. Maria is a variant of Mary, meaning star of the sea, though a Russian interpretation also adds obstinacy and rebellion. Olga means dedicated to the gods, holy. Finally, Anna is derived from the Hebrew 'Hannah', the mother of the Old Testament prophet Samuel, and means favour or grace. Whilst on this subject Ivan is a variant of John and means god is gracious.

When the three sisters were at home with Ivan they represented the first three goddesses in the hymn that Mahalakshmi created, namely: Mahakali, Mahasaraswati and Lakshmi, whom the great goddess first created. They represent the three gunas, forming an equilateral triangle, prior to the birth of creation. In the next part once they leave home and find partners in the form of Brahma, Vishnu and Shiva, the triangle breaks its symmetry and forms the circle of manifest creation.

One day, not long after, Tsar Ivan was taking a leisurely walk in the palace gardens, enjoying the beauty of the day with his three sisters. Suddenly, out of nowhere, a black cloud appeared and covered the entire sky. Thinking that they would probably need somewhere to shelter, Ivan instructed his sisters to retreat to the inside of the palace before the storm began.

As soon as they all stepped inside the palace, lightning flashed across the entire sky, thunder rattled the land and rain covered the entire kingdom. Before they knew what was happening, a falcon flew through a window. The moment he landed he turned into a handsome prince. He instantly lost his heart the moment he saw Maria, and asked Ivan for her hand in marriage. Ivan saw his sister staring starry-eyed at the handsome prince and accepted the proposal. The two young people were married shortly thereafter. After the wedding ceremony the prince promptly changed back into a falcon and carried his bride back to his kingdom.

This represents the first of several stages during which each of us steps down from the sphere of the divine into relative existence. The Russian idiom for losing one's mind or changing one's state of consciousness is always through the entrance of a storm.

Many ancient cultures venerated the falcon, particularly ancient Egypt, where it was regarded as the king of birds due to its strength, beauty and high flight. It was the sacred animal of the sun god Ra. Horus was also shown as a human with a falcon's head. In Peru, the falcon shared the same solar significance as a brother of the Incas and also a human ancestor.

Nearer home, in Norse mythology, the topmost branch of the 'world tree' is called Lerad, the peace-giver. On its topmost branch sat an eagle and on the eagle's beak, between its eyes, sat a falcon. The tree itself was known as Yggdrasill – the tree of knowledge of life, fate and the universe.

The first daughter in Indian philosophy would be Saraswati, the goddess of knowledge and the shakti, or active aspect, of Lord Brahma the creator. In addition to this, in another Russian story, a falcon named Finist is associated with the golden egg of creation – the hiranyagarbha – which the hymn says was created by Saraswati and Lord Brahma. Also bearing strong similarities to Peruvian mythology, Lord Brahma is regarded as the father of mankind, so it is quite conclusive that the falcon is taken to be the creator in this story. As well as being the goddess of knowledge, Saraswati also is the one that brings desire into relative existence.

One year to the day, Ivan found himself walking through a palace garden with the remaining two sisters. Just as had happened the previous year, a black cloud appeared and Ivan and his sisters ran back to the palace to escape the storm. When they got back to the palace the storm arrived, but this time an eagle flew in and turned into a handsome young prince. He looked at Olga, then Ivan, and asked for her hand in marriage. Ivan approved, as did Olga, and they were quickly married, after which the eagle carried Olga back to his kingdom.

The eagle also was widely regarded by many ancient cultures as the master of the air because of its speed, power and perception of the animal world. It was also a symbol of storm and thunder as well, thus combining the heat of the sun and the nourishing and fertilising qualities of the rain.

The vehicle of Lord Vishnu, the preserver and sustainer of the universe, is the eagle Garuda. The name Olga means dedicated to the gods or holy. Both epithets apply to the original creator in the hymn. It is said that Lakshmi brings beauty to the beautiful. She represents harmony in all things.

As before, it was exactly one year to the day when Prince Ivan was once again walking in a palace garden with his youngest and only remaining unmarried sister, Anna. The same turn of events occurred as in the previous years. Once again a thunder storm ensued and they had to rush inside to shelter. As soon as they got back inside the palace, a raven appeared, immediately after the storm had started. As soon as it landed it turned into a handsome prince. He looked at Anna, then Ivan, and asked for Anna's hand in marriage. Ivan did not hesitate in giving them his blessing and Anna did not hesitate in accepting the proposal. They were married and the raven carried Anna off to his kingdom.

The qualities and preferences of the raven certainly fit Shiva. His two most well-known aspects are as the king of yogis who prefers to sit and meditate in the wide open spaces of the Himalayas and whose main role is that of destruction and dissolution. Similarly ravens like to live alone and thus become a symbol of self-imposed solitude – and they are often associated with death, destruction and loss. Ravens are sacred to both Shiva and Kali, who likes to meditate in cremation grounds.

This rather puts a dent in Shiva's CV, until one examines what is meant by destruction and dissolution. Outwardly it is usually taken as being taken as involving the end of a great cycle when all of creation devolves back to its source for the great sleep of pralaya. In actual fact the dissolution is much nearer to home than that and it is central to what these stories are really about – namely to dissolve the shadow of the cloud of the false personality created by the ego back into the source of all existence, where doubt, duplicity, disease and death don't exist.

Tsar Ivan now lived alone in his immense palace, lonely and without a family to look after. He missed his sisters so much that one day he told his princes and boyars that he was leaving the kingdom in their care and that he was leaving for an indefinite period of time.

He mounted his horse and rode off. He rode up to a field of a slain army of soldiers. This army happened to have been defeated by the army of Marya Morevna, which was resting in a field of white tents. There he met Marya and made it clear to her that he came in peace. She invited him into her tent for a feast and he ended up staying with her for three days and nights. Both realized that they were madly in love and set a date to marry in Marya's kingdom. For years they lived happily and in peace.

The immense palace where Ivan lived is the infinite vast of the formless Absolute, of which the Vedas *say only one quarter takes the form of creation; the other three quarters always remain formless and unseen. He is leaving to begin his cycle of births and deaths before returning. His first port of call is to become united with his atman – the essential energy and driving force of evolution of everybody and everything in the universe.*

One day Marya came to Ivan and told him that she was going to have to leave to do battle with an army in another portion of her kingdom. When she departed she told Ivan that he was in charge of the kingdom until she got back and that he was not to enter the chamber at the tallest turret in the castle under any circumstances.

This is another version of the tree of wisdom or good and evil. As such it is an enticement to savour the fruits of desire and thus act against the divine commandments.

There is a charming piece in the Bhagavad Gita *which explains this rather well. It says:"Two birds are perching in the same tree – one does everything whilst the other sits and watches."*

The Veda *attaches great importance to human beings. It says: "You are part and parcel of that consciousness of the same source of divine energy. You embody the entire universe. You have come to the earth for a particular purpose – you are simply a traveller passing through. You are not the mind or the body."*

In the turmoil of 21st century life it is almost inevitable for us to read it as the one doing all the work being us while the Atman or inner guide sits quietly and watches. This level of understanding is almost inevitable when we are almost overwhelmed with actions needing to be done and those needed to be done in the near future.

However, there is another side of the coin. It first came about when I was playing cricket as a young man. At the time I seemed to be playing several levels above my class. Beautiful, well-timed cricket shots were disappearing to the boundary and people were clapping the shots. They said afterwards that it was the best innings I had ever played.

The truth was very different. I had done nothing at all. I was the observer watching my body move into position to play all these incredible shots and yet getting all the praise for doing absolutely nothing at all.

As I continued regularly practising Maharishi's self-development programmes, the same thing begin to spread in my teaching and particularly the poetry I appear to have written.

"What has this to do with the story you are analysing?" I hear you ask.

Well everything actually. Like Ivan in the story there must have been a time –many lives ago – when all of us were faced with the choice of remaining an observer or tasting the fruit of our actions, and we chose the latter. It is then that the intellect makes the mistake of thinking that we are the author of our actions. Whilst the choice is certainly ours, it is nature that carries out the action.

If our level of understanding of the laws of the universe is less than perfect, we inevitably make the wrong choice and then suffer from it, along with everybody else with whom we are connected. This is the first of a whole chain of errors that brings our level of awareness and understanding down lower and lower. The more we try to swim against the tide of Nature, the harder our life becomes.

While Marya was gone, Ivan wandered the castle for days, looking into every room and wondering when his love was going to come back. He remembered that in the tallest turret there was something inside that he was not supposed to see. Burning with curiosity he ran to the uppermost chamber in the turret and unlocked the door. Inside he found a giant lying sprawled on the floor with his arms and legs chained to the floor with seven iron chains.

The giant pleaded to Ivan that he had neither had food or drink for many years. Ivan, feeling pity, brought the giant a pail of water, which the giant drank in one gulp. He asked for two more pails and when he finished the last one he got up and broke through the chains like they were paper-thin. This was no ordinary giant: this was the one and only Koschei the Deathless.

He told Ivan that he would never see his wife again and flew out of the window like a whirlwind. Koschei flew across the land and swept up Marya, who was returning home from battle, and carried her off to his kingdom.

The tallest turret in our heads is the brain. It doesn't create consciousness as modern scientists believe – Maharishi says it acts as a piece of hardware, reflecting the pure unconditioned consciousness that drives the universe. However, once we have made the mistake of thinking we are both the author and executor of our actions, the sure hand of Mother Divine becomes hidden from our human awareness and as a consequence, the ego is allowed to run rampant through every field of action in our lives. Thus we become the one in chains, because all of our actions become subservient to the mind and body – and this creates a curtain obscuring all the gods from our awareness.

Ivan was depressed and he sat in the castle crying and weeping for his mistake and the loss of his love. Time passed and his wounds healed but he still missed his wife, so he decided to go to rescue her.

Fortunately we have a heart as well as a mind. Although it speaks a different language it can put us right by using our feelings. Something always comes along in our life that makes us take stock and change direction.

It doesn't appear in the story but Ivan must have learned to turn his mind inwards towards its source because the next three stops on his journey correspond with three different awakenings.

He rode on his horse for three days and on the third he saw a beautiful castle in front of him. Next to him, perched on an oak tree, was a falcon, which at the sight of Ivan flew down and turned into his first brother-in-law. They went inside the castle where his sister Maria was there to meet him. Ivan stayed with them for three days and told them that he had to leave. He left his silver spoon with them so they would know how he was doing and rode off on his horse.

Trees were often seen as axial pillars joining everything in creation with its source, thus symbolising a state of unity. All of the major cultures of the ancient world held the oak in high esteem. To the Greek, Roman, Celtic, Slavic and Teutonic tribes the oak was foremost amongst venerated trees, and in each case it was associated with the supreme god in their pantheon, oak being sacred to Zeus, Jupiter, Dagda, Perun and Thor respectively. Each of these gods also had dominion over rain, thunder and lightning.

In India it is seen that the cosmos is a great tree whose roots are in the underworld; its roots and trunk in the earth where mankind live and move; and its branches in the heavens where the gods reside and administrate the laws of creation. The Taittiriya Brahmana *puts it this way: Brahma was the wood with which the gods shaped heaven and earth.*

The sacrificial spoon in Hindu ritual is both an attribute to Agni the god of fire, who in turn offers up the oblation to the akasha for Lord Brahma. The oak was sacred to the thunder gods of Greece, as well as the Scandinavian and the Slavic countries.

He rode on further for three days. On the third day he came upon another castle that was more beautiful than the first. Looking at the immense structure he sat on his horse next to a large oak. In the oak was perched an eagle, who upon seeing Ivan flew down and turned into the second brother-in-law. They went inside the castle and met with Ivan's sister Olga, who was delighted to see him. Ivan stayed in the castle for three days and said that he would have to depart because he was on a quest to find his wife Marya Morevna. To see his progress the two asked Ivan to leave his silver fork. He did as he was asked and rode off.

A silver fork would no doubt be the trident. It is the traditional weapon of both Durga and Shiva; the symbol of all of the gods; and the union of past, present and future. Most importantly for Ivan, our spiritual traveller, it represents the destruction of the three root poisons: anger, desire and sloth.

Riding non-stop for a further three days, Ivan came upon another castle that was more beautiful than both of those he had stayed at before. In a large oak was perched a falcon who swooped down to Ivan and turned into the third brother-in-law. He invited Ivan in and Anna, the youngest of the sisters, embraced Ivan since she had not seen him in so long. Ivan spent three days with them and rode off, leaving them a silver tobacco box so that they could keep track of his progress.

The journey of the mind in meditation, as it goes deeper and deeper to its source, becomes increasingly serene and blissful. As it does so, two of the main nadis or nerve channels in the subtle body – often depicted as snakes either side of the shushumna – climb ever higher towards the thousand-petalled lotus, where Shiva as pure consciousness resides.

Silver stands for Ida on the left – the feminine principle of emotional refinement – resulting in purity, chastity and eloquence. On the other side is the golden pingala, representing silence, wisdom and incorruptibility. As the old saying goes, though one may have a golden tongue, silence is golden!

As before, Ivan left a tobacco box as a talisman so they would know how he was getting on. Modern tailor-made tobacco, although harmful to one's medical health, is not noted for its status as an hallucinatory drug but in the hands of a shaman it has been found to be both stronger and very effective in giving spiritual experiences to the novitiate, as is shown by a quote from The Encyclopedia of Psychoactive Substances *by Richard Rudgley, Little, Brown and Company (1998).*

'Whilst tobacco (Nicotiana spp.) is certainly a stimulant, in sufficient quantities (such as those used traditionally by American Indians) can have what, for all intents and purposes, may be called hallucinogenic properties. Certainly the South American Indian shamans see it as such, but this appears not just to be due to cultural conditioning (apprentice shamans are instructed beforehand of the nature of the visions they are going to see) but also to the actual chemistry of tobacco.'

Ivan travelled for three more days before coming up to the kingdom of Koschei the Deathless. Ivan bravely walked into the palace grounds and found Marya Morevna, who warned him that Koschei was out on a hunt. Ivan took Marya on his horse and rode off with her, hoping to make it home.

Koschei, returning from the hunt, was informed by a horse of his that Ivan had taken Marya. Hearing this news, he mounted the magical horse and caught up to Ivan and Marya in a flash. Koschei swept up Marya and told Ivan that he would not kill him, since he had taken pity on him in the past.

It is difficult for humankind to know the truth because, although it is the wellspring of our being, it is imprisoned within the three cages of the body, mind and intellect. We have to get past them and their boss – the ego – before we arrive on the doorstep of the one we seek. Whatever desire we have in our heart can be counteracted by the guile of the ego. The first time Ivan tried to be reunited with his true love, it was the call of the body, in the form of sight, smell, taste, touch and hearing, which was the cause of his failure.

Dejected, he sat on his horse and thought about his defeated effort. Driven to have his wife back he rode back to Koschei's palace to once again rescue Marya.

When he found Marya again she warned him that Koschei would be back soon. He ignored her warning and took her and charged off on his horse.

Koschei came back and was informed again by his horse that Ivan had taken Marya again. Mounting the magical horse he caught up to the two escapees just as fast as he had done previously, took Marya, and told Ivan that if he was ever to do that again that he would be killed.

This time it would be the sphere of the mind and emotions that would be the cause of his failure.

This time Ivan returned and waited several days, until Koschei left the palace again, to go in and rescue Marya. Ivan found

Marya and he told her to get on the horse and ride off with him. She was reluctant and he told him that he would be killed if Koschei found them again. Ivan told her that it was better to be dead than not to be with her and she responded by getting on his horse and riding off with him.

Koschei returned and found that Marya was missing and galloped after them in a fury. He caught up to them, grabbed Marya, sliced Ivan into many small pieces, and put the pieces into a tarred barrel, which he threw into the deep blue sea.

Ivan's third encounter with his inner enemy is in the form of the intellect. No matter how strong our beliefs are, the intellect can slice them up and mix them with a contrary message and easily turn strong belief into doubt.

The message of Ivan's third encounter with his ego is that his doubts had triumphed. His faith and belief were in tatters. The image of a tarred barrel filled with his dismembered body and dumped into the blue sea means that his ego had cast him adrift on the sea of birth, death and rebirth forever.

This is a description of the ritual death in the ancient mystery religions and mirrors the dismemberment of Osiris by Set in the mysteries of Isis.

As this was happening, the spoon, fork and tobacco box all turned black. The brothers-in-law all realized that something very terrible had happened to Ivan. The eagle flew to the sea, snared the barrel and carried it to shore. The falcon flew off to obtain the water of the living and the raven flew to obtain the water of the dead. The falcon and the raven flew back to the eagle, which was waiting for them. The three of them broke the barrel and put Ivan's body back together piece by piece. Next the raven poured the water of the dead on the severed pieces and they fused back together. Then the falcon poured the water of the living on the body and Ivan sprung back to life. Ivan thanked his brothers-in-law and walked back to Koschei's palace.

Brothers-in-law should be replaced by brothers-in-consciousness because all beings are linked in the heart with the source even though we are largely unaware of this. The condition of each of the talismans was a testament that things were not going well so the masculine aspect of the three goddesses came to his aid.

The fusing together of all the disparate pieces is reminiscent of one of the three main initiations of initiates in the ancient mystery religions, which is identical with an advanced spiritual state, which Maharishi calls cosmic consciousness. It is a cumulative process which builds up with each meditation. An individual following a realised guru will be given a technique that facilitates contact with the fourth state of consciousness called turiya, or transcendental consciousness as Maharishi calls it. Modern science has proved conclusively that this exists and is different from the waking, dreaming and deep sleep states of everyday life, both on the level of bodily chemistry and the electrical brain wave patterns that identify and characterise each of the individual states of consciousness. Regular contact with this changeless transcendental field of pure bliss cultivates the mind and body so as to enable one to be able to remain grounded in transcendental bliss consciousness even whilst engaging in dynamic activity with the outside.

This gradual, cumulative process links the individual with the cosmos as a whole, thus extending their sphere of influence and it results in the fully blown state of Cosmic Consciousness. Anybody who rises to this state is really great because he or she is really at one with the universe and has thus transcended their identity as a limited individual and now lives life in tune with the highest moral and ethical laws that run the universe. That is why this was called a ritual death in the mystery religions of the ancient world.

In the context of this story, Ivan the initiate has been elevated to being an integral servant of the cosmos. His mind is able to entertain each thought as its source, whereas most people can only appreciate an impulse from the source of their being at a relatively gross state after many modifications. That is why we humans make such a lot of mistakes. Ivan has been made anew. Although he would look the same outwardly, he now acts as a servant working in concert with the powers which run the universe with such skill and precision.

The ritual death is really a grand awakening to the proper order of things. One could compare Ivan emerging from being imprisoned within the triple cages of body, mind and emotions into a sphere of being one with the universe as being reminiscent of a beautiful butterfly emerging from its dowdy cocoon.

As such it takes him out of the sphere of cause and effect which keep us all trapped in the cycle of death and rebirth.

When Koschei left in the morning, Ivan sneaked inside, found Marya and told her to find out where Koschei had acquired his magical horses. When Koschei returned, Marya waited for the opportune time and asked him the question. He answered that he had got the horses from Baba Yaga, who lived on the other side of the River of Fire, which his magical handkerchief had helped him cross.

Anybody who has ever watched a conjurer will have guessed that his silk handkerchief is indispensable to the act. It is interesting that Koschei – whose alias is the ego – has one in this story. The truth is that the ego is the magic handkerchief because it is the seat of illusion that hides us all from reality. His magic handkerchief on the screen of the mind blots out Brahman – with and without form – from our awareness.

The magical horses are the sidhis or superpowers as listed and described by Patanjali. As the senses are often described as runaway horses in sacred literature, I am sure this was the original intention of the story. There are many of them but if I list just a few you will have a good idea of their scope and power:

Perfection of the body
Complete mastery over the sense organs
Complete mastery over nature

The ability to attain anything one desires
The ability to bring other people under your control
Make oneself infinitely large or small
To be able to fly through the air
To become invisible at will.

As the story of the Frog Princess came before this story, you will already know the true identity of the original pre-Christian Baba Yaga, so I won't go through it all again. Only to say that she is Brahman – both with and without form – as per the title of this particular folktale.

However, just to emphasise this point we will talk about the River of Fire. One of the many great things that Maharishi did in his lifetime was writing his Apaurusheya Bhashya, *a commentary on the* Rig Veda. *The first word of the* Rig Veda *after the bindo OM is Agnim, the god of fire. The rishi or cogniser is Ahamkara or the ego. Thus in order to get to Baba Yaga, one has to cross the river of fire. Everybody who does a puja to one or more aspects of Brahman or god has to invoke the goddess or god by lighting an oil burner or candle whilst chanting their own particular Gayatri Mantra to establish proper contact. This again shows the identity of the original Baba Yaga very clearly.*

Another good example is the beginning of the Durga puja I chant each morning, after chanting the opening Gayatri Mantra. It says:

Om agni jyoti
(the Divine Fire is the Light),

ravi jyoti
(the Light of Wisdom is the Light),

candra jyoti
(the Light of Devotion is also the Light…).

While Koschei slept, Marya took his magic handkerchief, gave it to Ivan and told him to go to Baba Yaga's house on the other side of the River of Fire.

Ivan started off for Baba Yaga's house and soon enough he was at the River of Fire. He waved the magic handkerchief and a crystal bridge rose up from a low and decrepit bridge and he was able to cross safely.

Crystal signifies spiritual perfection, whilst a bridge is the junction or a point of crossing from one plane to another or a change of state. Thus the crystal bridge is a telling description for the journey of the mind from the world of form to the transcendental pure consciousness.

Ivan walked and walked and was very hungry. He came upon a mother bird with her young. He thought of having them to eat but the mother bird told him not to eat them because he might need their help later, and Ivan trekked on.

Still famished, Ivan came up to a beehive from which he wanted to take some honey. However the queen bee flew to him and said not to eat any honey since he might need her help in the future, and so he walked on.

Not having eaten for a long time, he crossed paths with a lioness and her cub. Ivan wanted to kill the cub for a meal but was told not to by the lioness since he might need their help someday, and he walked on.

Every genuine spiritual traveller follows the path of ahimsa or non-violence to all their fellow creatures. Having purified himself through many years of meditation, Ivan would also find that almighty nature would support all of his actions.

He walked, long exhausted from severe hunger, and eventually made it to Baba Yaga's house. He met with her and told her that he would serve her. She told him that he could tend her stables, but if one horse escaped she would cut off his head and put it on a stake next to all of her other heads. She would reward him if he could manage to keep her horses at bay. She made him a hearty meal, told him to eat and sleep, and that he would be starting his work in the morning.

From a normal point of view, cutting off his head would sound pretty threatening, but seen from the background of sacred literature it is the normal expression for annihilating the ego. It is described this way in the Durga Saptashati, *through the extinction of Ravana in the Ramayana and the death of Kansa by Krishna. It must also be remembered that the goddess Kali wears a belt and a necklace of skulls of her devotees, all of which have surrendered their free will to her.*

The horses are his five senses. Whilst they are tethered in the absolute they do not move. Only when let loose in the relative creation do they try to gallop away into the field of desires.

In the morning, before waking Ivan, Baba Yaga told all of her horses to run away from Ivan once they got in the meadow.

After Ivan woke he took the horses as instructed to the meadow. As soon as they arrived all the horses ran off in different directions. Ivan could do nothing as he sat in the middle of the meadow. Then the same birds that Ivan had spared swooped out of the sky, forcing all the horses back to their stables.

Baba Yaga was angered at her horses and asked them what happened. They told her they had had no choice because the birds would have plucked their eyes out. She instructed them next time to scatter into the deepness of the forest.

Ivan woke up the next day and took the horses out and they ran into the depths of the forest as soon as they had the chance. The same lioness, her cub and an army of lions ran into the forest and chased the horses back to their stables.

Baba Yaga was once again angry at her horses when they were back in their stables. This time she told them to hide in the blue sea once Ivan took them out.

Ivan woke up and took the horses out, and sure enough they ran off into the blue sea. Then a swarm of bees flew at the horses that were standing in the sea and stung them until they returned home. One of the bees flew to Ivan and told him to go back to Baba Yaga's house and hide in the stables. The bee also told him to find a mangy-looking colt and flee at night. Ivan did as he was told and rode off on the ugly colt towards the River of Fire.

It is interesting to examine the true nature of Ivan's helpers. Birds have long been known as symbols of angels, with the ability to communicate with the gods or to enter into a higher state of consciousness.

The lion Simha is the vehicle of the great goddess Durga. A devotee lucky enough to have daily contact with her has his or her wilder instincts tamed and prevented from being led astray by the wild horses of desire. Being the vehicle of Durga, the lion also stands for dharma. Thus a devotee acting as a vehicle of Durga always acts in accordance with the highest aspects of dharma and is therefore free from sin.

Bees symbolise immortality, chastity, divine industry and order. They are also considered to represent the stars and winged messengers of the gods. In addition, they also obediently serve their queen, like Ivan in this story.

He reached the River of Fire, waved the handkerchief, and crossed the crystal bridge that appeared out of nowhere. The next morning Baba Yaga found that Ivan had taken one of her colts and she rode after him. When she came up to the River of Fire she tried to cross it, but fell in and was never heard from again.

When Ivan led his colt out into a pasture it suddenly turned into a strong and beautiful steed. Ivan mounted him and rode to the palace of Koschei the Deathless. Once he reached the palace, he found Marya Morevna, put her on his new magical horse and rode off.

Koschei found out from one of his magic horses that Ivan had come back and taken Marya. Furious, he mounted one of the horses of desire and charged after them. When Koschei caught up to them Ivan's horse struck Koschei in the head and killed him with that blow. Marya mounted Koschei's horse and she and Ivan rode back to their kingdom, stopping to feast at each of their brother-in-laws' castles.

The ego found out from one of the senses that Ivan and Marya had reunited, and tried to divide them in the same way as he had always done before, but this time it didn't work. He was wiped out by the fleetness and swift decision of a purified mind.

Tsar Ivan and Marya Morevna had unified their two kingdoms of the absolute and relative fields of life and also extinguished the great enemy of illusion. From then on they lived happily ever after.

The Wee Little Humpbacked Pony (Intro)

This title is a little conundrum in its own right and has a far different meaning from a story about a quaint little horse with a humped back, normally aimed at children. Let us take it apart piece by piece.

First of all, 'the' means the one and only.

'Wee' is an adjective both describing and emphasising the smallness of 'little'. Maharishi has often pointed out the importance of the words Anoraniyan Mahato- Mahiyan as defining the truth of the fullness of life. Anoraniyan is the transcendental reality which lies beyond the most subtle aspect of creation and exists as the true self of each individual. Mahato-Mahiyan is also not only larger than everything in creation but also the transcendental reality that lies beyond creation. In fact the source of creation is Anoraniyan and it continues to evolve until it becomes Mahato-Mahiyan. The entire phrase is often summed up as 'the smallest of the small is also the largest of the large'.

To the logic-bound mind still clinging to the boundaries of the intellect – which separates everything and divides it into categories – this would sound like gibberish. How can the largest and the smallest be the same? Put another way, the transcendental reality gives rise to both the microcosm and the macrocosm. That sounds more acceptable and understandable because science has got round to believing that a unified field underlies the four main forces in creation; but it hasn't yet got round to accepting it as the transcendental reality, because it cannot be measured by machines but it can be experienced by the mind.

Next – a hump is a protuberance rising above a level plane. The level plane is the abstract unchanging plane of the transcendental reality that gives rise to everybody and everything in the protuberance or 'hump' called relative creation. It is the same as what the Vedas say, namely: three quarters transcendental absolute, one quarter relative creation.

Lastly we come to 'pony'. As the charioteer of the body it would have to be very small but without it nobody would be able to move a muscle. But why talk of horses at all? Because in the traditional religious literature of the past chariots were drawn by horses so it was quite natural to use them as to symbolise sources of energy and power.

Thus the sum total of *The Wee Little Humpbacked Pony* is the one and only source and creator of everything in existence – the transcendental reality which underlies all existence and is present as the personal internal guide of us all, in the form of the Atma.

The Wee Little Humpbacked Pony

Once upon a time, in a land few people today ever walk, where birds and beasts could sometimes talk, in a kingdom full of wonders, humbly lived three young brothers.

In the 5th century BC, Empedocles described the tone of life in the golden age when human beings and animals understood each other and men, birds and animals glowed with kindly affection towards one another. Similarly, the Mahabharata attests that everybody was in tune with their inner self and were not only honest, truthful and free from want and disease, but also beheld the gods and great prophets. When this tale was conceived, only a few realised sages could emulate the people of the legendary golden age.

One year the brothers were faced with a vexing problem: something was trampling down their fields of wheat and ruining their harvest. So they decided to take turns standing watch at night to catch the culprit. The two older brothers stood guard the first two nights, but hid in fright when storms and cold winds blew through the fields.

The fields in question would be those of the mind and soul. The true objective of all our lives is to be able to harvest the fields of knowledge, bliss and happiness in a single lifetime. The current knowledge of a particular time is never enough. Unless it is in Sat Yuga – known as the golden age – knowledge is never complete and therefore open to doubt and error. It is necessary to be connected by a proficient master to our inner guide. It is only by going deep into oneself that such knowledge and experience will be gained.

According to Lord Shankara, true seekers need to have three essential attributes: the ability and courage to be able to think for ourselves; to have complete freedom of thought to inquire about our inner beings; and thirdly to have self-confidence and faith in our own judgement.

The youngest brother, Ivan, considered the fool of the family, would have preferred to sit in a corner singing songs at the top of his voice instead of taking his turn.

The songs he would be singing, or more likely chanting, were Vedic hymns to his ishta devata – his inner guide. It was this presence of mind that gave him the ability to see what the two surface levels of the mind had missed.

But once out there, Ivan stuck to his duty, and under the moonlit sky, saw what was doing the damage – a young horse with a snow-white coat. Ivan managed to jump on the animal, which immediately darted every which way trying to shake its unexpected passenger off. But Ivan tenaciously stayed on, even though he was riding front-to-back and holding on to the animal's tail!

The description of the horse as young and snow white tells us that the white horse is invariably a solar symbol of light, life and illumination. Their scope in ancient societies was almost limitless, ranging from the knowledge of heaven and earth, life and death to light and darkness. There is another aspect about this particular white horse, which makes this story very different and special from all the others.

About every 12,000 – 13,000 years a special event takes place in the universe. It is the birth of a new golden age when an old, corrupt, war-torn age based on materialism makes way for a spiritual age of peace and plenty, in which high levels of consciousness are the foundation of life, without crime and illness and so on.

This is further emphasised by the word 'young'. Like the return of spring after the harshness of winter, it means a return to the highest levels of natural law, when total knowledge and truth prevail.

There are four different ages: a golden age, when 100% of truth, peace and prosperity prevails; a silver age, still very advanced by our standards, when consciousness falls by 25%, making the institution of religions necessary; a bronze age when morality falls by 50%; and finally an iron age, where all the aspects of dharma have fallen to only 25%.

At this time we are in a time of transition, when the worst and shortest age is making way for the return of the golden age. At such a time the earth is highly populated to give people the opportunity to evolve spiritually and thus be assured a place in the new and better age.

A time of transition is also a difficult time which brings with it wars, natural disasters and global changes, eliminating those souls still clinging to harsh, cruel, animalistic behaviour. They will be found a new place in the universe where they can take birth and evolve spiritually.

By riding front to back, it means that Ivan had been given a meditation technique, which begins with a concrete name and sound, which would undergoes any number of subtle changes before arriving at its source in the transcendental awareness of the absolute.

Eventually the horse surrendered, but promised that if he were to be set free, he would give Ivan two golden-maned steeds of unheard-of beauty and a pony with two humps on its back and yard-long ears. Ivan could sell the two steeds, if he wished, but he should never part with the pony, who would be a true and loyal friend. Ivan agreed because he liked the idea of having the pony as a friend. (Being a fool, Ivan didn't have many friends.) Ivan then went home, but didn't tell his brothers exactly what had happened.

In actual fact the white horse and the two gold-maned horses symbolise three rays of the most important subtle energy sources which affect the well-being of our planet. Although the earth has countless connections of cosmic rays with the rest of the universe, these three are more important than any others. They connect the earth with the sun, the centre of the Milky Way and the centre of the galaxy. We could call them the solar ray, the galactic ray and the universal ray.

The earth receives an abundance of masculine energy from the sun; the galactic being brings an abundance of rays of feminine energy, ensuring that the natural evolution of minerals, plants and animals is maintained and thus providing a proper foundation for human existence. The galactic being also initiates a new zodiacal age every 2160 years, by sending out nourishing rays of celestial fire, which gives everything a transitional boost. In addition, the galactic being balances the more active and dynamic rays coming from the solar being.

The white horse symbolises the most important of these rays – the ones emanating from Lord Brahma, the creator of the universe. As soon as evolving souls reach the human stage of development they are initiated into the light of pure consciousness. As soon as the first day of human civilisation dawns on the earth, the Universal Being presides over human evolution. He does this through the Divine Messenger. The ray he sends is pure chitta, capable of awaking the light of pure consciousness in everything. He is especially interested in individuals who have prepared themselves to receive it. The Creator takes a special interest in enlightened human souls because they are deemed his own children.

Every 12,000 – 13,000 years the Creator emanates his own life force into the smallest grain of matter on this planet. The entire world becomes filled with spiritual light.

At such a time the whole of the earth wakes up and assumes its proper role in the cosmic order of the universe and the floodgates are open to human awareness and a new golden age dawns on the earth.

These rays across the universe also have their counterparts in each individual. The solar ray is called the pingala, the feminine galactic ray is the ida and the power from the source itself is the shushumna.

Needless to say, the description of the pony is figurative because it is really Ivan's inner guide – the Atman. 'Having ears a yard long' is still used as an expression to state that one has heard all the neighbourhood gossip, but in this case it means everything ever said by anyone, which can only be the Atman, as he has accompanied every creature, human and divine that ever lived.

Days later, one of the brothers wandered into the shed and discovered the two golden-maned steeds and the humpbacked pony. "So this is why my fool brother has been sleeping in here lately," he thought. He and his brothers then decided to sell the horses in town, split the profit, and not tell Ivan.

"Let that fool search for them all he wants," they said.

The two brothers are the senses and the surface mind. They wouldn't have had the nous to realise that Ivan had been meditating and not sleeping. Also they wouldn't have been aware that the two horses with golden manes could not be sold. They are often depicted as snakes that rise from the muladhra chakra and criss-cross the shushumna three times on their way up to the third eye or ajna chakra.

It wasn't long before Ivan discovered the two steeds missing and the humpbacked pony told him what had happened. The pony told him to jump on his back, though, and that they'd chase the brothers down. The pony was small but it was as fast as lightening! In a flash, they overtook the thieves. Ivan called to them: "Shame on you, my brothers two. It might well be that you are smarter than me, but stealing horses from you is something I'd never do." The brothers apologized, but said that the family desperately needed the money. Trusting as he was, Ivan believed them, agreed to sell the horses for the family's sake, and accompanied them to town.

Seeing that every character in the story is an aspect of the hero or heroine it would be impossible to take them away, but they can easily be taken to a more gross state of awareness. As the two elder brothers represent the senses and the surface mind, we can take it that the two steeds were harnessed to a much more gross state of awareness than Ivan, who is the buddhi – the spiritualised intellect. Thus they were easily brought back to be the focus of attention.

Soon it became dark and they all decided to rest. Suddenly they noticed a strange light in the distance and Ivan was coaxed into investigating it. Riding the pony toward the light, Ivan saw an entire field illuminated as if it were day! And all the light came from a bright glowing feather from the fabled firebird. The pony warned Ivan not to touch it or trouble would come his way. But Ivan picked up the feather anyway and put it under his hat. When he returned, he told his brothers that the light went out before he got there, and said nothing about the feather.

A feather symbolises truth in its entirety. The light of truth is the enemy of darkness – the first light of dawn banishes the entire darkness of night. The ultimate truth far transcends what is taken to be truth by people of the world, thus it becomes secret knowledge. Hence the well-known phrase for keeping a secret – keep it under your hat.

The next day they all arrived in the city to sell the golden-maned steeds at the fair. The Tsar got word that two magnificent animals were for sale and went to take a look at them. He fell in love with the beautiful horses and bought them at once. But as the Tsar's grooms began to lead the horses off, the horses reared up, broke free from their bridles, and went back to their master, Ivan. Seeing the horses' allegiance to the boy, the Tsar was compelled to ask him to work in the royal stable, an offer which Ivan accepted. But he demanded that he wouldn't be beaten and that he be allowed to sleep all wanted.

It is impossible to be parted from the two gold-maned steeds and still remain living. It is not surprising that the king fell in love with them because they would be united with the home of knowledge – the ajna chakra. Knowledge is also equated with light. It is a well-known fact that one ray of the first light of the dawn is sufficient to dispel the entire darkness of the night sky.

Ivan did a good job in the stables, although his singing drove everyone crazy! The royal chamberlain, whose duties as head stableman had been given to Ivan, was more than a little annoyed though. He had it in for the young lad and watched him closely for mistakes. One day, as he was spying on Ivan, he almost shrieked in horror when he saw a brilliant light coming from the room. Ivan, of course, had taken out the feather. The chamberlain reported back to the Tsar that Ivan was purposely hiding the feather and that the boy had bragged that he could get the firebird itself anytime he wanted.

Ivan's singing would actually be Vedic mantras because they are part and parcel with his meditation technique of gradually bringing about the transformation that would make him divine.

When he was called in before the Tsar, Ivan denied everything, but became tongue-tied when the Tsar opened a small chest and showed him the feather. Ivan begged for forgiveness. The Tsar said that he would forgive him if Ivan brought the live firebird back to him. Otherwise the boy would be flogged and tortured to death!

Poor Ivan left the palace in tears and told the humpbacked pony of his problem. The pony offered to help, saying: "The tasks here are really quite small, and I'll assist you with them all. First place in separate troughs millet and wine, then we'll get going and you'll be fine."

In eight days they reached a meandering brook which stood before a majestic hill made of pure silver. The pony said that this was a favourite watering hole of the firebirds and instructed Ivan to mix the millet with the wine and put it out for the birds. Sure enough, at midnight the birds arrived and ate the concoction. When one became a little woozy, Ivan grabbed it, put it in his sack, and rode back to the Tsar.

The eighth day of both the waxing and waning moons is sacred to Durga – the organising aspect of Mother Divine. In India they still have the lunar calendar, to which this day refers. It is the half-moon stage in both halves of the lunar month – which may be considered as transcendental days because the moon is neither rising or setting at these points.

According to Robert Cox, the term 'meandering' is a loose translation of helissetai – meaning moving in a spiralling helix, the upward movement of the ida and pingala through the chakras – the feminine and masculine energies of the sun and moon.

The hill made of silver must refer to the ajna chakra. The story says that firebirds often go there because it is their favourite watering hole. They stop there because it is the last but one chakra before going on to the thousand-petalled lotus. This would be the final stop of the firebird as it brings with it the elixir of immortality.

The firebird symbolises cosmic pure awareness and is thus able to ascend and descend the ladder of creation. Like the fabled birds: Garuda, the phoenix, Quetzalcoatl and the Bennu bird of ancient Egypt, firebirds rise from the ashes of the departing age to herald a new and better age.

When Ivan came into the palace with his catch, the bird's light was so intense that the Tsar started to call for help, thinking the room was on fire!

"There are no flames here," Ivan assured him. "The light is from the fabled firebird."

The Tsar was so amazed at what he saw that he made Ivan his personal valet.

It was no wonder that the Tsar was frightened. I will quote a few lines from the Danadikam, *written in praise of Garuda, so as to say something about the appearance of a firebird:*

'That splendorous group of red rays appear at that time..... Garuda sparkles in that flood of red light.

Your other heroic deeds stand out like the mighty winds that sweep the universe during the time of the great deluge.

Your wings in flight generate mighty winds that stir up all the oceans and make them flow over their boundaries. The waves that rise and fall from those powerful winds reach down to the netherworld (Pathalam) and the effect is like a violent blow given by the palm of one's hand.'

We can see that although a new and better time is coming, it is also a time of planetary upheavals, when the imbalances caused by people upsetting the natural rhythms as consciousness declines after Sat Yuga have to be corrected. Thus many deaths follow as a consequence, as recorded in the great flood at the end of the last period about 13,000 years ago, which wiped out the entire antediluvian civilisation.

As with the three rays there is an individual aspect to Garuda as well as that of the universal. The poem also shows that he can confer the knowledge of the Veda to his devotees and also takes the form of the five pranas, or aspects of breath, which underlie all the systems of the body and keep it healthy.

The royal chamberlain was now more incensed and jealous than ever. He swore he'd get back at the lad.

Several weeks later the chamberlain heard servants in the kitchen reading a fairy tale about 'a tsar-maiden, pretty and young, whose mother was the moon, and whose brother was the sun'. The chamberlain told the Tsar all about the girl and how Ivan had boasted that he could get her anytime he wanted. The Tsar was so enamoured with the story that he just had to have the girl for himself. So he called on Ivan to bring her in... or off with his head! Ivan once again left the palace in a horrible state. But his pony promised to help him find the maiden.

The two left the palace and on the eighth day reached the ocean shore where the maiden was known to appear several times a year. Following instructions from the pony, Ivan set up a tent with dinner and sweets inside so that he could capture her when she walked in to sample the food. Sure enough, the next day the maiden arrived in her small boat and went to the tent, just as the pony had predicted.

Once again Ivan set off on the eighth – transcendental day – to find the pretty tsar-maiden whose mother is the moon and whose father was the sun. This description depends on which way you are looking at it. From the viewpoint of the human individual, climbing the ladder of perfection, it is correct. However, from the point of view of the descent of the divine into manifestation, she is Lalita – the source of everything there is. We are all playing a part in her lila – her divine play. Ultimately everything that has happened, is happening at present and will happen in the future is unreal.

The story infers that she can be tempted with tasty food. However she is most accessible to worshipers of the sri chakra and her one thousand names – the Lalita Sahasranam.

Ivan looked through a hole in the tent and thought to himself that the girl was too pale and thin for him. Then she began playing the gusli and humming a melody so sweetly that Ivan closed his eyes and fell asleep. He lost his chance that day to grab her, but succeeded the next day, and the three of them went back towards the Tsar's palace.

The gusli is an ancient Russian zither, whose full history is unknown. It has a strong, resonant, sweet and even silvery sound with a long duration.

The old Tsar saw the beautiful tsar-maiden and begged her to marry him. She refused. But that only made him want her more, so he kept asking. Finally, in order to end this incessant pleading, she told him that she would marry him if he would bring to her a ring lost somewhere on the bottom of the ocean.

Ivan was called in once more to do this seemingly impossible task, again under threat of death if he failed. As Ivan was leaving the palace, the maiden called to him and told him to be sure to convey her greetings to her mother (the Moon) and her brother (the Sun), and to ask why they had been hiding from her for three days now.

Ivan and the pony started their search for the ring at the ocean shore, where they encountered Chewdo-Youdo, a huge monster whale who had been beached there for ten years. Poor Chewdo-Youdo was barely alive. Holes and scars ravaged his body. A growth of trees had sprouted on his tail. There was even a small peasant village on his back! The huge whale looked sadly at Ivan and implored him: "If you see them soon, please ask the Sun and Moon why I am being punished so. And then I can perhaps help you find the ring, you know."

So Ivan and the little humpbacked pony rode off to see the lovely Moon who lived in a crystal palace with pillars of gold.

Ivan passed on the greetings from her daughter, the tsar-maiden, and asked why the Moon and Sun had been hiding their rays for three straight days. The Moon unexpectedly broke down in tears, hugging Ivan and kissing him on the cheek. "What a relief to know she's alive!" she said. "The Sun and I have been grieving under dark clouds because we thought she was lost!" Ivan told her the whole story and about the fact that the Tsar wanted to marry her.

That the world had been in darkness for three days harks back to the spate of natural disasters at the end of an age of iron before a new golden age begins.

The Moon was quite upset with this news because she knew the Tsar was old enough to be the maiden's grandfather. "Tell her," she said, "that someday a young, handsome gentleman will come and marry her and she'll be free of the toothless Tsar. Tell her also that I love her and will always be with her."

Ivan ended his visit with the Moon by asking why Chewdo-Youdo was being made to suffer. She said he was being punished because he had swallowed three dozen ships. "If he lets the ships go, we will take away his woe."

The whale is symbolic of his karma load. It is beached because the karma is the sum of all of our unfulfilled desires, debts and wrong doings, that keeps bringing us back in different bodies and different places. Once this has been cleansed by the fire of tapas, one is free from all affliction and becomes one with the eternal source.

Ivan bade the Moon farewell and went back to Chewdo-Youdo. In his defence, the whale said he had swallowed the ships only to protect himself. But no matter – with a mighty roar, he opened his gargantuan jaws... and out sailed three dozen ships, people and all! The wounds on the whale suddenly healed and, like in the old days, Chewdo-Youdo thrashed the water with his tail, free at last. He then promised to help Ivan find the lost ring. He put the sturgeon in charge of the mission, and soon the ring was found!

Arriving at the kingdom, Ivan handed it over to the Tsar, who, likewise, presented it to the tsar-maiden. But she still refused to marry him. "I'm only fifteen," she said. "How could we possibly wed? All the other Tsars would laugh. They'd say, 'The old fool is marrying his granddaughter!'" But she said that he could regain his youth if he dipped himself in three cauldrons: one with boiling water, a second with boiling milk, and the last with ice water.

Often the Tsar is equated with the transcendental absolute but in this story he represents the vain ego. In the worship of the sri chakra, Lalita is also fifteen, but as she is in the field of the absolute beyond time she always stays young and youthful even though her lifespan is beyond human comprehension.

The Tsar had the cauldrons prepared in his courtyard. The next day he ordered Ivan to jump in to test them. "If you don't do this for me, I'll chop you into little pieces!" Ivan, naturally, was quite frightened. But his little humpbacked pony was there and before Ivan jumped into the boiling water, the pony dipped his muzzle in each cauldron, sprayed the boy with a shake of his head, and whistled three times.

The three cauldrons would be the three main nadis in the subtle body. We know that the spiritual marriage is the ida and pingala becoming unified by the presence of the risen kundalini. When this happens, devotion dawns and the role of the ego is greatly diminished.

Now Ivan went in. There was a hush as Ivan remained underwater in the last cauldron for what seemed like ages. Then... out he came, magically transformed into the most handsome and debonair of men!

By transformed, the original version would have been that he had been spiritually and mentally transformed but not necessarily his outer appearance.

This encouraged the Tsar so he threw off his own clothes, jumped in, and boiled to death in the very first cauldron.

The tsar-maiden took Ivan by the hand. Ivan no longer saw her as pale and thin, but rather as the most beautiful and delicate girl ever to walk the Earth. Later the two were married with great pomp and ceremony. And they were also unanimously sworn in to lead the kingdom! Everyone lived happily ever after, including the humpbacked pony who forever remained Ivan's true and loyal friend.

THE TALE OF FINIST THE FALCON

Many years ago there was a rich, widowed merchant who had three daughters. The two elder daughters were only interested in parties and clothes, but the youngest, Marya, took on the duties of housekeeping for her father.

This tale follows in the same tradition of the greatest analogical story – the great Indian epic, the Mahabharat Thus, like its famous ancestor, all the characters in the story are aspects of the human psyche. In fact it is one of the Russian versions of Cinderella. Obviously there have been some minor changes that further mask its original intent, but this is to be expected, considering the vast time it has been in existence, plus the fact that its real meaning has been lost for probably thousands of years. It is a tribute to the Russian people that it has changed so little during the 5,000 years of its existence.

The father is the ego. He fulfils the desires of each of his children, who symbolise the hierarchy of the mind. It is divided into two camps. The two elder daughters symbolise the choices made by the powers of darkness. They always tend to face towards the external environment for the gratification of the senses. On the other side is the younger daughter Marya representing the forces of light. She is what is known as the buddhi, whose function is always to discriminate so as to follow the path of choosing that which is morally correct and best for her spiritual evolution.

In fact Marya is an excellent name for the spiritually seeking aspect of the mind. Like names such as Mary and Maria it means the star of the sea. In Hindu philosophy the sea is called samsara

– meaning the restless cycle of birth and death – exactly what Marya wants to escape from.

This version is slightly different from the Western Cinderella in that the desires of the two elder daughters are grouped together, whereas in the Grimm's version they are described as having different desires because they represent the change of quality of the gross external world of the senses to the deeper more reflective qualities of the intellect. However, this version does the same thing a different way, inasmuch as the desires of the two elder daughter represent the surface mind with their first wish and become deeper each time

Finally, Marya, the youngest daughter represents the spiritual yearning of the psyche, so it is quite natural for her to spend her life serving others. All the tales I have read from any country always have the younger child as the one seeking unity with the divine source. In a physiological sense she is the same age of course, but like the initiate the tale had been written for, the spiritual dimension came later.

One day the merchant was going to the local market and asked his daughters what presents they would like him to bring them. The two elder daughters asked him to bring them expensive new fabric for dresses, but Marya humbly said, "All I want, dear father, is the feather of Finist the Falcon."

The elder daughter's first wish characterises the surface of the mind which relates to vanity and anything in fashion in the outer environment, which makes the individual stand out and impress other people as being special. Marya has only the one spiritual desire – to have a feather from the firebird Finist the Falcon.

The firebird in Slavic tales plays the same role as the kundalini in tales originating in the Far East. They both have the same function in common – they sit at the base of the spine, asleep in most people. What makes them rise or rear up is a suitable spiritual practice that awakens them and gradually purifies the mind by transcending the relative phase of existence and giving it access to deeper, more subtle areas of existence.

In actual fact the feather is not the whole bird but it leads one to it. Marya asks for a simple mental technique that will take her mind to the source. This echoes Cinderella's 'sprig or branch from the tree of knowledge'. She knows that just 'one feather' – probably a mantra – is sufficient to light up the whole room of her mind and make it enlightened.

Each time the technique takes the mind to the unmoving transcendental field of life, the body gains a great deal of rest, allowing the accumulated stresses to unwind as thoughts. As soon as the initiate is aware that he or she is not thinking the mantra, it is time to go back to it and allow the transcending process to begin again. It is the release of stress that allows the firebird Finist to rise up like a phoenix through the internal chakras of the spine.

When the father came home from the market, he brought new beautiful fabric for his eldest daughters, but he told his youngest daughter that he could find no one at the market who had ever heard of the feather of Finist the Falcon.

It is not surprising that such a feather was not available at the market nearest to home because it was the field of the five external senses.

On his next trip, he went to a market much further away from his home. His elder daughters asked him to buy them new silk scarves, but Marya again asked only for the feather of Finist the Falcon. Again he brought home expensive presents for the elder daughters, but no one at the market had ever heard of the feather.

This time, the more distant market is deeper and further away from the surface mind. Again the desires of the two external phases of the mind could be met but was not a place where a spiritual technique was available.

When the merchant next planned to go to market, this time at a great distance from home, the elder daughters asked for new earrings, and Marya asked only for the feather of Finist the Falcon. In the market he found beautiful earrings for the elder daughters. On the way back he met an old man with a small box in his hands.

However at the third market, representing the deeper aspect of the mind, things were different. Not only could it fulfil the more shallow regions of the mind in the form of earrings but as he was thinking of leaving that field of thought, a sudden wave of inspiration from an even deeper part of his mind broke through.

"What do you have in the box, good man?" asked the merchant.

"The feather of Finist the Falcon," the old man replied.

"Please, sell it to me," begged the merchant.

The old man replied, "This feather is not for sale, but I can give it as a present to a kind man, as you are."

Spiritually enhancing techniques cannot be bought, they have to be earned. The man he met before coming home would have been sent by his inner guide, who is aware of all our actions. He or she steers our course through life and brings us into contact with all the people and problems we have to work through to complete the outstanding pile of karma we have brought with us. We have the opportunity of working it through and wiping the slate clean or of piling up further problems, which will have to be put right in another lifetime. Kindness and helping others, plus the desire to have a full spiritual life, are the necessary qualifications to enable the wiping clean to take place.

When he returned home with the feather, Marya thanked him with great joy and ran into her room to open the box. She took out the feather, waved it in the air, and a falcon appeared. She rapped on the floor, and the bird turned into a handsome young man. They talked happily with each other far into the night. The elder daughters thought they heard a man's voice in her room and knocked on the door, demanding to come in. Before they could get in, however, Finist flew out the window. Breaking into the room and finding no one there, the sisters were very annoyed and left it, filled with suspicion.

Marya was overjoyed because a feather from Finist the Firebird and Cinderella's sprig from the cosmic tree of knowledge both symbolise the same thing – both are inseparable from the source that gave birth to them. Each would be the correct Sanskrit mantra to bring them a fullness of understanding. All Sanskrit mantras have the totality of knowledge within them because 'A' was the first letter to emerge at the birth of creation, so it carries the totality of knowledge within itself. It is also the key that allows each word to be pronounced.

It is a tribute to Russia that the Russian version of the tale has not strayed too far from the original meaning: 'rapping on the floor' is a sign of this. It is said that the process of meditation starts in the throat chakra and descends through the other four chakras to what is commonly called the kundalini, but in the case of Russia they call it the firebird or the phoenix.

The rapping on the floor symbolises the need for the firebird or kundalini to rise up and purify the five chakras or worlds of the senses. We all carry within us the seeds of impure desires which are going to cause us a great deal of trouble in the future because they are not in accord with the sanatana dharma of how we should behave.

What happens when we meditate is that the phoenix rises up through the gross chakras to the finer ones as the mantra takes us to the transcendent. Day after day this process continues, so gradually the seeds of latent desires are roasted so they are unable to sprout. In actual fact, 'firebird' is an excellent term with which to describe this process.

Finally, when it reaches the sixth chakra, often called the third eye of spiritual eye, the mind leaves the ever-changing world of the senses and comes to the junction point of the ever-changing relative and the never-changing field of the absolute, underlying creation.

The conversation which the elder sisters heard would be the unwinding of stresses, caused by the deep level of rest the body gains by taking the mind back to the unmoving transcendental field. In fact it mirrors what we experience every night when we are unconscious, where it is the value of deep sleep which promotes the release of stress, which we experience as dreams of life.

Every night for the next three nights, Finist flew in through the window to visit Marya when she took the box out and waved the feather. But on the third night the two wicked sisters saw him leaving. While Marya was out, they stuck sharp knives and needles into the window frame. Marya did not suspect anything and that night, while waiting for Finist, she dozed off. When Finist tried to enter the room he flew into the sharp objects, which cut him and injured his wings, so he called sadly in to her, "Good bye, my dear. If you love me, you will find me." And he flew away...

Not just three nights but twice every day, the same process is repeated and yet every time it seems like a different experience. The window is the junction point of a house and the outer environment; in this case it symbolises the mind at the brink of the absolute. The mind in harmony with its divine source causes the ascending one into the ever-ascended beloved. The sharp instruments that would stop him from being reached are thoughts in the form of doubts or criticisms, such as "Why are you wasting your time meditating when you could be doing something more useful in the house or garden or going down the pub or watching the telly?"

I remember the day I learned TM. I was given the mantra and shown into a darkened room. I began to silently think the mantra, when a similar thought came on the scene. What it said was very brief and to the point – "Is this a con?". Suddenly the part of me which is Marya made me realise that I couldn't feel my hands. That was sufficient to tell me that something unusual and different was happening, so I went back to the mantra and never looked back.

In the morning Marya discovered the knives covered with blood on the window frame. She wept and called out to Finist. When there was no answer, she decided to go to find her sweetheart. She walked for days and days through the forest and finally came to a small hut.

It soon becomes clear that a short period of meditation twice a day not only makes you feel happier and healthier but one's passage through the day and the world of work is much smoother, so the doubts disappear and one continues on the path of light.

An old woman came to the door, and asked her, "Where are you going, my beauty?"

Marya answered, "To find Finist the Falcon."

"Oh, it's a long way," said the old woman. "I will help you. Take this silver plate and golden egg. Don't give them away for money, but trade them for a word with Finist."

The age of the woman was old beyond conception but nevertheless she would look young and very beautiful. She is the innermost aspect of everybody and everything in the universe. She is Mother Divine – the source and organiser of everything in creation. When she appears in one form or another, it is only after the mind has been purified. The tray is silver like the moon and represents the mind, whilst the egg is golden and symbolises the heart.

Marya took the present, thanked the old lady and continued on her journey. She came to two more small houses, where the sisters of the first old woman entertained her and gave her two other presents – a golden needle and a golden spindle. Finally, Marya came to a palace. She heard that Finist was there and that the princess of the land wanted him to marry her. Marya went to the kitchen and begged for work as a servant and was hired to do scullery work.

Here things become a little blurred. When these wisdom tales later fell into the hands of storytellers their aim shifted from being an easily remembered sequence of stages of spiritual advancement an initiate could expect to pass through, into a medium of amusement and wonder to amuse crowds of people. Hence changes and misunderstandings were bound to take place. Whenever there were three seemingly similar occurrences in a tale they would be grouped together as happening on three consecutive days, the storytellers being completely unaware that they should be separated by periods of many years.

Being hired for scullery work at a royal palace actually means that the initiate had risen to the state of cosmic consciousness. The regular infusion of Transcendental Consciousness over a period of time cultures the mind to accommodate simultaneously both the stillness of the transcendental source of life and the ever-changing field of relative existence. When this goal has been reached it is possible for the initiate to become the devotee-cum-servant of one of the celestial gods. It is the path of purifying the senses and emotions which terminates in the state of God Consciousness. This explains the significance of the golden egg, which symbolises the purified heart and should have come much later than the tray.

Treading the path to God Consciousness is truly wonderful. An initiate is always in a state of love towards his or her given aspect of the deity and this is returned in no small measure. One is given tasks to carry out each day and the path through life becomes very smooth and filled with love.

One evening, after a long hard day of work, Marya sat down and played with the silver plate and the golden egg. The princess happened to see her and immediately demanded that Marya sell her these rare treasures. Marya, remembering the advice of the three old women, replied, "I cannot sell them. But if you let me speak to Finist the Falcon this evening, I will give them to you as a gift."

The princess agreed, but she was suspicious so she put sleeping powder in Finist's supper. Later that evening Marya went to Finist's room and started to call to him: "My darling, Finist the Falcon, wake up."

But he was fast asleep and could not hear her.

Here things become a little blurred – the princess is really a celestial goddess, whose realm is the finest level of relative existence. They are often called gods but they are actually the administrators of the universe, who carry out their role in accordance with the will of God. In fact, since the initiate as

Marya has probably been assigned a devata, she is doing the same. There is no question of Finist being drugged. The reason that Marya as an initiate cannot see her beloved at this juncture is because she is not yet sufficiently awake to realise his presence within her.

The next day the same thing happened: the princess saw Marya playing with the golden needle. On the third night, when she had won the right to speak with him by giving up the spindle, she entered the room and knelt by his bed as she called to him, but he again had been drugged and could not hear her.

Knowing she had lost her last chance, she began to cry, and one burning tear fell on his cheek. This time he felt her sorrow, opened his eyes, and exclaimed, "Dear Marya, I am so glad to see you again!" She told him all about her adventures since they had last met. They embraced each other and fled from the princess's palace. When they came back to Marya's house, they forgave Marya's sisters, married and lived happily ever after.

The needle and the spindle are significant instruments for joining things together. Similarly, once an initiate has reached the state of God Consciousness, this is very near the end of the spiritual journey and is called Unity Consciousness. It is at this point when the form of the beloved moves to cement a marriage or inseparable union with the seeker. This is why most tales end with 'and they both lived happily ever after'.

Wee Little Havroshechka – Intro

Anybody sufficiently lucky enough to be following a realised guru will know of a particular time when meditation is most effective. It is between 3.30 and 4.30am and is known as the Brahmi Muhurta.

As the term suggests, it is a time when pure consciousness and the finest aspect of relative creation coexist. Brahmi is the name of the most ancient form of Sanskrit text. The gospel of St. John opens with 'in the beginning was the word and the word was God'; the same word and the same sequence of sounds in the *Vedas* creates everything there is in the universe. The Brahmi Muhurta almost certainly relates to the time in India when consciousness became matter, because it is the greatest repository of Vedic knowledge of earth, even in this dark age.

At such times the meaning of complex problems and philosophical ideas can be seen in their proper light, so what was before an insoluble metaphysical problem becomes transparent.

It was at such a time that the revelation of a wisdom story called Havroshechka came to mind.

The essential difficulty of this story is that it has been personified to such an extent that the personality has become uppermost. Whilst this is confusing at first, it is necessary because it mirrors what happens to us as the feeling of a separate human being takes over from our true nature – pure consciousness.

The word Havroshechka means 'tiny small'. To the initiate it would mean what Maharishi calls the junction point between the never-changing absolute and the ever-changing relative phases of existence. We can call this the initial seed from which everything grows, or alternately the golden egg containing the master plan for the total knowledge of all creation.

Late in the last century, Maharishi ran knowledge courses called Total Knowledge and Perfect Man. He said it would be possible to acquire total knowledge in one brain if we could occupy the fort from which all things stem.

The appellation of the name makes it difficult to get beyond words like 'little' and 'wee', or both together as in 'little wee Havroshechka'. This is because it represents the point where the smallest of the small is the seed which becomes bigger than the biggest – or to put it another way, the location of the infinitesimal seed which is the master plan that creates the infinite universe.

What the story is really saying is that the three children are really emanations or states of mind which have developed from pure consciousness as consciousness becomes formed as an individual. The difficulty arises because the order of emanation has been reversed so as to make the story make sense. Actually three eyes should come first as they correspond to the junction point of consciousness and matter.

Maharishi has shown us that it is both easy and possible to reach that state through the process of transcendental meditation. As with other revelations it occurred when waking from sleep, where one emerges from the formless into form. There is an interval between sleep and waking, or transcendental consciousness and the waking state, when these revelations take place. They can also take place in the countryside or places of natural beauty in which the mind becomes quiet and still.

At the junction point both coexist for a short while. Any creative person will tell you that if the material is not recorded quickly it will evaporate and no longer be available to the waking state.

Wee Little Havroshechka – the Story

There are good people in the world and some who are not so good. There are also people who are shameless in their wickedness. Wee Little Havroshechka had the bad luck to fall in with such as these. She was an orphan and these people took her in and brought her up, only to make her work till she couldn't stand. She wove and spun and did the housework and had to answer for everything.

Now the mistress of the house had three daughters. The eldest was called One-Eye, the second Two-Eyes, and the youngest Three-Eyes. The three sisters did nothing all day but sit by the gate and watch what went on in the street, while Wee Little Havroshechka sewed, spun and wove for them and never heard a kind word in return.

Havroshechka was an orphan in the sense that she was really a child of Mother Divine. Her real home – as it is for all of us – is in the absolute realm of complete bliss and happiness. She was a stranger to relative creation. As the Vedas and the scriptures say, 'we are not the body or the mind'.

The mistress or stepmother is relative creation and her three daughters are increasingly subtle aspects of the mind. The three children – One-Eye, Two-Eyes and Three-Eyes – are degrees of wakefulness. Keshavadas sums it as 'stealing the kundalini for improper use'.

One-Eye represents the realm of the senses. Rather than getting caught up with creatures such as the Cyclops, I think it is better to stay with Plato who said that the Cyclops were beings typical of the original condition of uncivilized men. In other words, slaves to their senses.

Two-Eyes represents the intellect, which divides and classifies the whole field of life into tiny isolated and unrelated systems, thus completely losing sight of life's big picture.

Three- Eyes represents a much higher state of consciousness, called cosmic consciousness.

Sometimes Wee Little Havroshechka would go out into the field, put her arms round the neck of her brindled cow and pour out all her sorrows to the cow.

Who else could do everything for you but Mother Divine? She does everything anyway but as the desires of the ego make us identify with the action it causes us to assume that we are both the author and enjoyer, instead of being a witness to the play of the universe. The task of the wish-fulfilling cow is one of the tasks of the goddess Saraswati.

"Brindled, my dear," she would say, "they beat me and scold me, they don't give me enough to eat, and yet they forbid me to cry. I am to have five pounds of flax spun, woven, bleached and rolled by tomorrow."

And the cow would say in reply, "My bonny lass, you have only to climb into one of my ears and come out through the other and your work will be done for you." And just as Brindled said, so it was. Wee Little Havroshechka would climb into one of the cow's ears and come out through the other, and behold! there the cloth would lie, all woven and bleached and rolled. Little Havroshechka would then take the rolls of cloth to her mistress, who would look at them and grunt, and put them away in a chest and give Wee Little Havroshechka even more work to do.

And Wee Little Havroshechka would go to Brindled, put her arms round her and stroke her, climb into one of her ears and come out through the other, pick up the ready cloth and take it to her mistress again.

This is an interesting description of meditation. A specific mantra is whispered in one ear in relative creation and takes the mind down to its source and comes to rest in transcendental pure consciousness. During the passage of its journey down to the source, it undergoes definite changes in sound and subtlety as it passes from different levels of the senses, mind, intellect and feelings until it comes to rest in the source – Transcendental Consciousness. That is how a sound in waking consciousness can be transformed into Transcendental Consciousness. Finally the attention comes back to the relative creation – the other ear. One has the feeling of being totally rested and regenerated.

The more one does it the more automatic the process of life becomes. One can enjoy the outcome without becoming chained to it.

One day the old woman called her daughter One-Eye to her and said, "My good child, my bonny child, go and see who helps the orphan with her work. Find out the box who spins the thread, weaves the cloth and rolls it!"

We began the story of Marya Morevna with part of a hymn called the Pradanikam Rahasya to illustrate the births of the main Hindu gods and goddesses. Mahalakshmi was the first and created both Kali/Durga and Mahasaraswati, followed by another version of herself. Each of these three gave birth to a male and a female, which was the origin of the Hindu trio of Brahma/Saraswati, Vishnu/Lakshmi and Siva/Gauri.

Whilst it is not stated anywhere, the original three goddesses may well be the same as the Norns, the Moerae and the Three Fates, who spin the cloth of illusion of relative life. The names of the Moerae are Kolto (Clotho), Lakhesis (Lachesis) and Atropos. Kolto spins the thread of life from her distaff; Lakhesis determines the length of thread with her rod; and Atropos cuts it with her shears at the appropriate time of death. Thus by deduction Kolto may well be Kali, Lakhesis, Lakshmi and Atropos Saraswati. I think this is probably true because other traditions say that the three spinners are both older than the gods and are also responsible for their deaths.

Weight to this theory is added by Maharishi in his commentary on the first six chapters of the Bhagavad Gita. *He said that Mother*

Divine has the longest lifespan in relative creation so it was adopted by Veda Vyasa as the yardstick to measure the amazingly long lives of the gods in his historical epic, the Mahabharata. *Thus like Lachesis, Lakshmi is the rod by which other lifespans are measured. One is also tempted to say that the names are also not dissimilar. There is one sticking point, however, because in* The Chandi Path *Saraswati is usually taken to be the source of desires and also of their fulfilment.*

One-Eye went with Wee Little Havroshechka into the woods and she went with her into the fields, but she forgot her mother's command and she basked in the sun and lay down on the grass. And Havroshechka murmured, "Sleep, little one eye, sleep!"

In actual fact what is called little one Havroshechka in the story is really the atman – the inner guide who guides us to all the people and situations we meet in this life, so she is always with us all of the time. Although brindled normally means the patterns on the coats of animals, in this sense it is the drab, colourless, inner one that gives rise to all the patterns of life-forms in the universe.

One-Eye shut her eye and fell asleep. While she slept, Brindled wove, bleached and rolled the cloth of illusion. Consequently the mistress learned nothing, so she sent for her second daughter, Two-Eyes.

"My good child, my bonny child, go and see who helps the orphan with her work."

Two-Eyes went with Wee Little Havroshechka, but she forgot her mother's commend and she basked in the sun and lay down on the grass. And Wee Little Havroshechka murmured, "Sleep, little eye! Sleep, the other little eye!" Two-Eyes shut both of her eyes and dozed off. While she slept, Brindled wove, bleached and rolled the cloth.

The old woman was very angry and on the third day she told her third daughter, Three-Eyes, to go with Wee Little Havroshechka, to whom she gave more work than ever. Three-Eyes played and skipped about in the sun until she was so tired that she lay down on the grass. And Wee Little Havroshechka sang out, "Sleep, little eye! Sleep, the other little eye!"

But she forgot all about the third little eye. Two of Three-Eyes' eyes fell asleep, but the third looked on and saw everything. It saw Wee Little Havroshechka climb into one of the cow's ears and come out through the other and pick up the ready cloth.

The third eye is called the ajna chakra. It is known as the third eye – the eye of wisdom, the confluence of three main nadis or subtle nerve centres. They are called ida, pingala and shushumna. Incidentally, the ida is the quality of the coolness of the moon in our body and is associated with our mind, thought and harmony; whilst the pingala is the heat of solar activity and controls our movement, activity and consciousness. The shushumna flows when they meet in the ajna chakra – the confluence of the three inner rivers, Ganges, Yamuna and Saraswati.

The ajna is called the guru chakra – and the Eye of Shiva. The actual meaning if the word ajna is 'command'. It is through this chakra that the disciple receives commands and guidance from his guru and also commands from the divine, higher self.

It is the source of first thoughts and intuitions. Apparently it works as a kind of internal telephone direct from the muladhara chakra. It is generally thought to be more active in women than men but as yet there appears to be a lack of scientific information on this subject.

During the next part of the story it is important to keep in mind that the ajna chakra forms the boundary between human and divine consciousness.

Three-Eyes came home and told her mother what she had seen. The old woman was overjoyed, and on the very next day she went to her husband and said, "Go and kill the brindled cow."

The cow in question here is not an animal but it does symbolise the four main aspects of the Veda *– the* Rig, Sama, Yajur *and* Atharva Vedas.. *The* Veda *is not a set of ancient books containing the peace-loving, pastoral hymns of a very ancient agricultural society, as many academics view it. It is actually the sounds that* *create everything in the universe and is eternal and non-human – thus without origin.*

The cow is also known as the wish-fulfilling animal. It is cognate with the Veda. *Its four legs are said to be the four books of the* Veda *and the four teat holes, the source of all nourishment: physical, emotional, intellectual and spiritual. Large groups of pandits trained in chanting the Veda effectively are commissioned by people in India to overturn their ill fortune by appeasing the gods with specific rites in Sanskrit to appease the gods*

In Hinduism, the cow is a symbol of wealth, strength, abundance, selfless giving and a full earthly life.

The old man was astonished and tried to reason with her. "Have you lost your wits, old woman?" he said. "The cow is a good one and still young."

The old man would be the intellect. He doesn't like changes especially when his usual pattern of thought and the routine it lays down seem to work so well.

"Kill it and say no more," the wife insisted.

The wife is Divine Mother in form. She is only too aware that the old edifice has to be pulled down in order for a new one to be built in its place.

There was no help for it, and the old man began to sharpen his knife. Wee Little Havroshechka found out all about it and she ran to the field and threw her arms around the brindled cow.

"Brindled, dear," she said, "they want to kill you!"

And the cow replied, "Do not grieve, my bonny lass, but do what I tell you. Take my bones, tie them up in a kerchief, bury them in the garden and water them every day. Do not eat of my flesh and never forget me."

According to Maharishi, the most important phrase in the Bhagavad Gita *is verse 45 of Chapter 2, which says:*

The Vedas' concern is with the three gunas.
Be without the three gunas,

O Arjuna. Be free from duality, ever firm in purity, independent of possessions, possessed of the Self.

By self he means 'God within us', who is source of all existence, bliss and truth. What we normally take to be the self is a patchwork of likes and dislikes we have accumulated throughout our lives. Our entire life and our future plans are all centred around these. What Lord Krishna is saying to Arjuna is that one can never know the ultimate truth unless we go beyond the field of relative creation; neither can we be truly happy in relativity unless our thoughts and feelings are established in the blissful realm that lies beyond the sphere of relativity.

The old man killed the cow, and Wee Little Havroshechka did as the Brindled One had told her. She went hungry, but she would not touch the meat, and she buried the bones in the garden and watered them every day.

Of course it would impossible to kill Saraswati as the wish-fulfilling cow, but one has to do this figuratively in order to take the relationship to a higher level. Whilst the Veda *is the ideal template for life on earth, the* Upanishads *starts at the end of the* Veda. *All of the verses of the* Upanishads *are about realising the eternal inner truth within each of us. In actual fact all the old favours as the wish-fulfilling cow would continue in a form that would meet the needs of the new alignment.*

The bare bones of Saraswati would be her name in sound form, which the person would meditate upon. That would be sufficient to bring about the gradual transformation in consciousness, which in turn brings new levels of experience and knowledge to the individual.

After a while an apple tree grew out of them, and a wonderful tree it was! Its apples were round and juicy. Its swaying boughs were of silver, and its rustling leaves were of gold. Anybody in that vicinity would stop to look, and whoever came near marvelled at its beauty.

It is the tree that symbolises the entire universe, to which an enlightened person has become unified. It is called vanaspati because it brings forth fruit without producing blossom. This is why it is impossible to tell the difference outwardly between an enlightened person and an unenlightened one.

One day One-Eye, Two-Eyes and Three-Eyes were out walking in the garden, when who should chance to be riding by at the time but a young man, handsome and strong and rich and curly-haired. When he saw the juicy apples he stopped and said to the girls teasingly, "Fair maidens! I will marry the first one who can bring me an apple off that yonder tree."

Off rushed the three sisters to the apple tree, each trying to get ahead of the others. But the apples which had been hanging very low and seemed within easy reach now swung up high in the air above their heads. The sisters tried to knock them down, but the leaves came down in a shower and blinded them. They tried to pluck the apples off, but the boughs caught in their braids and unplaited them. Struggle and stretch as they might, they could not reach the apples and only succeeded in scratching their hands.

The other sisters could not reach the apples of love, immortality and happiness because they were in lower states of consciousness and were thus out of reach of the source.

Then Wee Little Havroshechka walked up to the tree, and at once the boughs bent down and the apples came into her hands. She gave an apple to the handsome young stranger, who married her. From that day on she knew no sorrow, and she and her husband lived happily ever after.

This kind of marriage is called the sacred marriage, when the ultimate object of lover becomes united with the lover; or to put it in another way, when the traveller who had lost their way through many lifetimes finds their way home and lives happily ever after.

Vasilisa the Beautiful

A merchant had by his first wife a single daughter, who was known as Vasilisa the Beautiful. When she was eight years old, her mother died. On her deathbed, she gave Vasilisa a tiny wooden doll with instructions to give it a little to eat and a little to drink if she were in need, and then it would help her. As soon as her mother died, Vasilisa gave it a little to drink and a little to eat, and it comforted her.

Her earthly mother died, but not the Mother of the Universe because she is the mother within all of us, whether we are aware of her or not. The doll that she gave to Vasilisa was actually a small replica of Mother Divine, such as Durga, Lakshmi or Saraswati, to be used for performing a puja each day. I am sure of this because the same thing happened to me in 2001, on my first visit to India. The food and drink she had to offer are a part of the puja Vasilisa would have performed every day.

After a time, her father remarried to a woman with two daughters. Her stepmother was very cruel to her, but with the help of the doll, Vasilisa was able to perform all the tasks imposed on her.

The Divine Mother administers the whole of creation, so it wouldn't be difficult to change the outcome of the karma that Vasilisa had brought with her into her new life.

When young men came wooing, the stepmother rejected them all because it was not proper for the younger to marry before the older, and no one would look at her ugly daughters.

Traditionally, a step-family is the family one acquires when a parent enters a new marriage, whether the parent was widowed or divorced.

One day, the merchant had to go on a journey. His wife sold the house and moved them all to a gloomy hut by the forest. One day she gave the girls all a task and put out all the fires except a candle. Then her older daughter put out the candle, and the two sisters sent Vasilisa to fetch fire from Baba Yaga's hut.

Baba Yaga was originally the Mother of the Universe in Vedic times, but with the inevitable decline in knowledge from its zenith in Sat yuga to its almost total demise in Kali Yuga, when human-kind's knowledge of the truth declines by 75%, she is believed to be some kind of scary witch, with a few good aspects.

In India 'Baba' is still a term of endearment, used to refer to a great and wise sage or guru. Yogananda and his Master both served Babaji, an avatar, who has lived in the Himalayas for thousands of years. In fact it was Babaji who chose Yogananda to be his ambassador to bring Kriya Yoga to the West. This took place because Jesus appeared to Babaji and asked him to send someone to the West to spread the message of Christianity, because although his followers still do good works, they have lost the ability to commune inwardly with God.

This makes me wonder if Babaji asked Brahmananda Saraswati to send Maharishi because the Virgin Mary told some children to pass a message on to some TM teachers from the USA, who were visiting St. James church in Medjugorje in the 1980's. The church was packed to the gills. They were in the midst of this great crowd. The children were up the front, their faces turned up listening and talking to the Holy Mother. Suddenly the children turned towards the congregation and pushed their way through the crowd until they came to the TM teachers. They said that Mary had a message for them. It was just three sentences: "Your Master – Maharishi – is the greatest living Master on earth at this time. All that he is trying to accomplish will happen. Also, Russia is going to become the greatest country in the world."

Similarly 'yaga' would have originally meant some form of devotional worship performed in front of a sacrificial fire, called a yagya. That is why Vasilisa was given a 'murti' – a representation of Durga or Lakshmi – to worship, which was later misunderstood as a doll.

The doll advised her to go, and she went. While she was walking, a feathered gargoyle rode by her, dressed in white and riding a white horse whose equipment was all white; then a similar rider in red rode by when the sun rose. Much later, another dressed all in black rode by.

These three riders all serve Baba Yaga and convey a dual purpose. Firstly, they are the three qualities known as the gunas in India and are present in every situation we face in our lives – but one always predominates. The red one is 'rajas' and symbolises desire and attachment through constant activity. The one in black is 'tamas', which stands for laziness, decadence and dissolution, and the one in white is 'satva' – meaning the good and positive values of truth, honesty and justice.

They also symbolise the three periods of the day: white is dawn and twilight, believed to be the best times of the day to practice meditation and devotional practices; red is the sunrise that brings constant light throughout the day, when we work and earn our living; and black brings the darkness when we rest and go to sleep.

She came to a house that stood on chicken legs and was walled by human bones. A black rider, like the white and red rider, rode past her, and night fell, but the eyes of the skulls lit up.

Vasilisa was too frightened to run away, and so Baba Yaga found her when she arrived in her mortar and pestle.

Baba Yaga said that Vasilisa had to perform tasks to earn the fire, or she would eat her. For the first task, she had to clean the house and yard, cook supper, and pick out black grains and wild peas from a quarter measure of wheat. The next morning the white rider and the red rider rode through the house.

Baba Yaga arriving in her mortar and pestle

Baba Yaga reminds me of Kali – the seventh form of Durga – who helps us lose our desire by replacing it with devotion. As you can see, Kali carries the fire of tapas or devotion that transforms our material egotistic desires into spiritual devotion wherever she goes. It is the element of fire that this takes place through meditation and worship.

Even in India, the sight of the skulls and the lolling tongue still frightens many people, but the country hasn't gone as far as turning the goddess into a witch.

Modern interpreters of the story have misunderstood the hidden meanings and have taken it literally. The 'house and yard' actually refers to her body and the room in which she does her worship. When I was invited to visit the Devi Mandir in California in 2012, on the wall of the washroom was the slogan: 'cleanliness is next to godliness!'.

Similarly, the fire is not the one that enables one to light the surroundings and cook, but the hidden inner fire of tapas that connects one with the celestial field by the agency of Agni.

Baba Yaga left, and the doll did all the work except cooking the supper.

It is a modern misconception that we do the work. In actual fact we have the intention and the powers of nature carry it out. Every day when I am doing puja, it would certainly look as though it was me but in reality it is the goddess herself who is stationed within me, chanting the mantras and manipulating the process; though if seen by an eyewitness, I am sure they would swear it was me.

When the black rider rode through the house, Baba Yaga returned and could complain of nothing. She had three pairs of hands seize the grain to grind it, and set Vasilisa the same tasks for the next day, with the addition of cleaning poppy seeds that had been mixed with dirt.

Again, the doll did all except cooking the meal. Baba Yaga set the three pairs of hands to press the oil from the poppy seeds.

The three pairs of hands are Vasilisa as the pujari and meditator, the goddess within and the agencies of nature in the physical universe..

Vasilisa asked about the riders and was told that the white one was day, the red one the sun, and the black one night. As Baba Yaga had cautioned her about too many questions, she did not ask about the hands, which, Baba Yaga informed her, would have meant she would have been seized by them like the wheat and the poppy seeds, for food.

Baba Yaga asked how she performed the tasks, and Vasilisa said it was with her mother's blessing. Baba Yaga wanted no one with a blessing in her house and drove her out, but gave her a skull with burning eyes as the fire she had asked for. The skull told her to bring it home.

She arrived home to find that her stepmother and stepsisters had been unable to light a fire since she left.

Her stepmother and sisters were actually her mind and senses, wedded to the desires of the material world.

The skull soon burned them up, and Vasilisa stayed alone, waiting for her father. She wove linen and gave it to the Tsar, but it was too fine for other women to sew, and so Vasilisa came to sew it, and the Tsar fell in love with her and married her.

Both her father and the Tsar were actually God. The marriage that gives rise to 'they lived happily ever afterwards' in most so-called 'fairy tales' takes place when a spiritual unity takes place between the worshipper and her object of worship – namely one of the forms of God.

It is fitting now that Vasilisa has reached her final spiritual goal to examine the significance of her name. Although it would be very different from the one it replaced after the collapse of the Vedic culture of Kievan Rus, the person responsible for this task was able to pass on a lot of secret information by choosing the name Vasilisa.

Although it is considered to be a feminine name in modern times, the two parts are a combination of the ultimate in royalty and leadership. Vasil is Greek for Basil- meaning kingly, honest, brave kind , trustworthy etc and Lisa means empress or queen.

Combined they form a brilliant description of the highest level of human evolution- namely Unity Consciousness- the masculine aspect of Lord Brahma and Saraswati the shakti that brings forth Creation.

The Clever Jackal

Once upon a time there lived a weaver whose ancestors had been very rich, but whose father had wasted the property which he had inherited in riotous living. He had been born in a palace-like house, but he now lived in a miserable hut.

The very rich ancestors of the weaver's family refer to the spiritual wealth of the far off age of Satya Yuga, called the 'golden age' when people lived in full accord with dharma, the laws of the universe, because their understanding was 100%. However, during the course of the descending yugas of time that followed, there was a slow but progressive loss of understanding until it reached rock bottom, at only 25% in Kali Yuga. Thus the comparison between his ancestors, who lived in a palace, and himself, who lived in a miserable hut is actually a metaphor comparing the abilities mind compared with bodies of people in Satya Yuga and Kali Yuga

Interestingly, Maharishi also refers to his technique of Transcendental Meditation as a means of regularly enhancing the features of a hut until it becomes a palace with the onset of full enlightenment, which is also the original meaning of this story.

The loss of the spiritual meaning in most folktales is one of the consequences of the progressive fall in understanding from the fullness of spiritual knowledge in Sat Yuga to its nadir in Kali Yuga. In this one, the term 'weaver' has been taken literally as a common tradesman, when in actual fact the weaver is an analogy for being well-evolved spiritually. We only have to remember that Patanjali called his yoga sutras 'threads' to know that as spiritual weavers are helped by Indra to become wedded to our inner ishta devata, who guides us home to be one with God.

Hard by the hut was the lair of a jackal.

From the gross material of the body to its finest aspect are the five elements of earth, water, fire, air and akash. It must be remembered that the holy seat of God is within us all at the point value where the absolute and relative universes meet.

The jackal, remembering the wealth and grandeur of the weaver's forefathers, had compassion on him, and one day coming to him, said, "Friend weaver, I see what a wretched life you are leading. I have a good mind to improve your condition. I'll try and marry you to the daughter of the king of this country."

"I become the king's son-in-law!" replied the weaver; "that will take place only when the sun rises in the west."

"You doubt my power?" rejoined the jackal. "You will see, I'll bring it about."

The jackal in this story must have originally been Indra. Indra has two roles – he is both the king of the gods and also our inner warrior who leads us from the prison of the body, in which we are ruled over by the demons within us, to the gates of enlightenment.

In the original story, the marriage, or a state of oneness, would have been to a goddess and not a princess.

The next morning the jackal started for the king's city, which was many miles off. On the way he entered a plantation and plucked a large quantity of the leaves from the trees in it.

There are 32 kinds of betel leaves. Each specie seems to have positive results on the human nervous system but he would have searched and chosen the leaves of the nagval – the sleeping creeper – because it is known to be linked with brahma loka – the home of the creator.

Nagval has the ability to attract certain frequencies of brahma loka and bring them to the earth. The leaves are in the shape of a heart and are thus called 'the golden heart of nature'.

The sattvic frequencies of the image of the deity are absorbed by the stalk, which results in creating subtle air, which is transferred to the tip of the leaf and into the atmosphere. These frequencies of refined subtle air have the ability to activate the will of the deity worshipped and purify the mental sheath of an embodied soul.

I would not be surprised if it was actually soma the jackal was eating in the original story. This was not soma grown in the outside world. It would have been produced within the body of the weaver to feed his inner celestial devatas. Maharishi said this happens once a person reaches cosmic consciousness, which is the stepping stone to higher states of consciousness. The ninth mandala of the Rig Veda *is full of hymns about producing soma to feed Indra – alias 'the jackal'.*

Their appealing leaves are a symbol of status and hospitality for greeting kings, nobles and guests in the cultural heritage of India.

He reached the capital, and contrived to get inside the palace. On the premises of the palace was a tank in which the ladies of the king's household performed their morning and afternoon ablutions. At the entrance to that tank the jackal laid himself down. The daughter of the king happened to come just at the time to bathe, accompanied by her maids. The princess was not a little struck at seeing the jackal lying down at the entrance. She told her maids to drive the jackal away.

It is at this point where the original meaning of the tale becomes completely lost because the realm of Satya loka, where all the gods reside, has been replaced by an earthly one and the joy of having an ishta devata to guide the weaver to achieve the state of God Consciousness has been replaced by gaining the hand in marriage of an earthly princess. As you will later see this princess turns out to be Mahalakshmi.

The benefits of being able to work with higher beings who know how to effortlessly work in tune with all the laws of nature and who can foresee the consequences of our actions cannot be underestimated.

Today, because of science we are currently both introducing new forms of life that probably shouldn't be here, whilst destroying many of those that should be.

Think what chaos could entail if a few rogue personalities could fly, become invisible and had the ability to create or destroy anything they chose?

The jackal rose as if from sleep and instead of running away, opened his bundle of betel leaves, put some into his mouth, and began chewing them. The princess and her maids were not a little astonished at the sight. They said amongst themselves, "What an uncommon jackal this is! From what country can he have come? A jackal chewing betel leaves! Why, thousands of men and women of this city cannot indulge in that luxury. He must have come from a wealthy land."

"Sivalu! Which country do you come from?" the princess asked the jackal. "It must be a very prosperous country if the jackals chew betel leaves. Do other animals in your country chew betel leaves?"

"Dearest princess," replied the jackal, "I come from a land flowing with milk and honey. Betel leaves are as plentiful in my country as the grass in your fields. All the animals in my country – cows, sheep, dogs – chew betel leaves. We want for nothing. Happy is the life we lead."

Where the jackal, alias Indra, lives is the innermost strata of life, where knowledge is always pure and adulterated. It is the home of the gods or angels who administrate creation in accord with the will of God.

The jackal opened his bundle of betel leaves, put some into his mouth, and began chewing them.

"Which country is that where there is such plenty?" asked the princess. "Your king must be a very happy man to rule over such a kingdom."

"As for our king," said the jackal, "he is the richest king in the world. His palace is like the heaven of Indra. I have seen your palace here; it is a miserable hut compared to the palace of our king."

The princess, whose curiosity was excited to the utmost, hastily went through her bath. Going to the apartments of the queen mother, the princess told her of the wonderful jackal lying at the entrance of the tank.

Her words excited the curiosity of the queen and the jackal was sent for. When the jackal stood in the presence of the queen, he began munching the betel leaves.

"You come from a very rich country," said the queen. "Is your king married?"

"Please your majesty, our king is not married. Princesses from distant parts of the world tried to get married to him, but he rejected them all. Happy will the princess be whom our king condescends to marry!"

"Don't you think, Sivalu," asked the queen, "that my daughter is as beautiful as a peri, and that she is fit to be the wife of the proudest king in the world?"

A Peri is an extremely beautiful maiden in Persian mythology

Sivalu is a Sanskrit word for jackal. In fact, this Russian version is exactly the same as one called 'The Match Making Jackal. In Bengal.

"I quite agree with you," said the jackal. "The princess is exceedingly beautiful. Indeed, she is the most beautiful princess I have ever seen; but I don't know whether our king will have a liking for her."

"Liking for my daughter!" said the queen. "You have only to paint her to him as she is, and he is sure to turn mad with love. To be serious, Sivalu, I am anxious to get my daughter married. Many princes have sought her hand, but I am unwilling to give her to any of them, as they are not the sons of great kings. But your king seems to be a great king. I can have no objection to making him my son-in-law."

The queen sent word to the king, requesting him to come and see the jackal. The king came and saw the jackal, heard him describe the wealth and pomp of the king of his country, and expressed himself not unwilling to give away his daughter in marriage to him.

After this, the jackal returned to the weaver and said to him, "Oh lord of the loom, you are the luckiest man in the world; it is all settled; you are to become the son-in-law of a great king. I have told them that you are yourself a great king, and you must behave yourself as one. You must do just as I instruct you, otherwise not only will your fortune will not be made, but both you and I will be put to death."

"I'll do just as you bid me," said the weaver.

The shrewd jackal drew in his own mind a plan of the method of procedure he should adopt, and after a few days went back to the palace of the king in the same manner in which he had gone before, that is to say, chewing betel leaves and lying down at the entrance of the tank on the premises of the palace. The king and queen were glad to see him, and eagerly asked him about the success of his mission.

The jackal said, "In order to relieve your minds, I may tell you at once that my mission has been successful so far. If you only knew the infinite trouble I have had in persuading his majesty, my sovereign, to make up his mind to marry your daughter, you would give me no end of thanks. For a long time he would not hear of it, but gradually I brought him round. You have now only to fix an auspicious day for the celebration of the solemn rite.

There is one bit of advice, however, which I, as your friend, would give you. It is this. My master is so great a king that if he were to come to you in state, attended by all his followers, his horses and his elephants, you would find it impossible to accommodate them all in your palace or in your city. I would therefore propose that our king should come to your city, not in state, but in a private manner; and that you send to the outskirts of your city your own elephants, horses, and conveyances, to bring him and only a few of his followers to your palace."

"Many thanks, wise Sivalu, for this advice. I could not possibly make accommodation in my city for the followers of so great a king as your master is. I should be very glad if he did not come in state; and trust you will use your influence to persuade him to come in a private manner, for I should be ruined if he came in state."

The jackal then gravely said, "I will do my best in the matter" and then returned to his own village, after the royal astrologer had fixed an auspicious day for the wedding.

On his return the jackal busied himself with making preparations for the great ceremony. As the weaver was clad in tatters, he told him to go to the washermen of the village and borrow from them a suit of clothes.

As for himself, he went to the king of his race, and told him that on a certain day he would like one thousand jackals to accompany him to a certain place. He went to the king of crows, and begged that his corvine majesty would be pleased to allow one thousand of his black subjects to accompany him on a certain day to a certain place. He requested the same of the king of the paddy birds.

In Indian legends, birds and animals act as vehicles for many gods and goddesses. In the original version of this tale, the intended marriage is spiritual and not external with a person from the opposite sex, so Indra – alias the jackal – would have invited a multitude of devatas.

The thousand crows would be his ancestors. Crows are still worshipped by Nepalese people on the first day of Diwali in modern times. Crows are believed to play a major part in linking the lives of the living with the dead. The practice is called Shradh. It takes place every year in India during the dark part of the lunar month called Ashwina and is called the fifteen days of the Pitru Paksha.

Paddy birds are often called java sparrows and symbolise the divine forces that keep everybody well fed. There is a legend that the people didn't have the right seed to sow their field so they sent a green bird up to the granary of heaven, where it was given the heavenly rice seed, which it brought back for the people.

A modern scientist has called it 'the one bird revolution'. Apparently, the secret of getting a bumper rice harvest is to release ducklings into the paddy fields soon after the seedlings are planted. Paddy birds don't eat the rice seedlings. They eat up insect pests and the golden snail which attack rice plants; they also eat the seeds and seedlings of weeds. They also oxygenate the water by using their feet to dig up the weed seedlings and so encourage the roots of the rice plants to grow.

At last the great day arrived. The weaver arrayed himself in the clothes which he had borrowed from the village washermen. The jackal made his appearance, accompanied by a train of a thousand jackals, a thousand crows, and a thousand paddy birds. The nuptial procession started on its journey, and towards sundown arrived within two miles of the king's palace.

There the jackal told his friends, the thousand jackals, to set up a loud howl. As soon as they heard this bidding one thousand crows cawed their loudest, while the hoarse screeching of the thousand paddy-birds furnished a suitable accompaniment. The effect may be imagined. They all together made a noise the like of which had never been heard since the world began.

While this unearthly noise was going on, the jackal himself hastened to the palace, and asked the king whether he thought he would be able to accommodate the wedding-party, which was about two miles distant, and whose noise was at that moment sounding in his ears.

The king said, "Impossible, Sivalu; from the sound of the procession I infer there must be at least one hundred thousand souls. How is it possible to accommodate so many guests? Please, arrange it so that only the bridegroom will come to my house."

"Very well," said the jackal, "I told you at the beginning that you would not be able to accommodate all the attendants of my august master. I'll do as you wish. My master will come alone in undress. Send a horse for the purpose."

The jackal, accompanied by a horse and groom, came back to fetch his friend the weaver and take him to the palace. He thanked the thousand jackals, the thousand crows, and the thousand paddy birds, for their valuable services, and told them all to go away, while he himself, and the weaver on horseback, wended their way to the king's palace.

The bridal party, waiting in the palace, were greatly disappointed at the personal appearance of the weaver; but the jackal told them that his master had purposely put on a mean dress, as his would-be father-in-law had declared himself unable to accommodate the bridegroom and his attendants coming in state.

The royal priests now began the interesting ceremony, and the nuptial knot was tied for ever. The bridegroom seldom opened his lips, adhering to the instructions of the jackal, who had been afraid lest his speech should betray him. At night when he was lying in bed he began to count the beams and rafters of the room, and said audibly,

"This beam will make a first-rate loom, that other a capital beam, and that yonder an excellent sley."

The princess, his bride, was not a little astonished. She began to think, "Is the man, to whom they have tied me, a king or a weaver? I am afraid he is the latter; otherwise why should he be talking of weaver's loom, beam, and sley? Ah, me! is this what the fates have kept in store for me?"

In the morning the princess related to the queen mother the weaver's soliloquy. The king and queen, not a little surprised at this recital, took the jackal to task about it.

The ready-witted jackal at once said, "Your Majesty need not be surprised at my august master's soliloquy. His palace is surrounded by a population of seven hundred families of the best weavers in the world, to whom he has given rent-free lands, and whose welfare he continually cares for. It must have been in one of his philanthropic moods that he uttered the soliloquy which has taken your Majesty by surprise."

The jackal, however, now felt that it was high time for himself and the weaver to decamp with the princess, since the proverbial simplicity of his friend of the loom might any moment involve him in danger. The jackal therefore represented to the king, that weighty affairs of state would not permit his august master to spend another day in the palace; that he should start for his kingdom that very day with his bride; and his master was resolved to travel on foot, only the princess, now the queen, should leave the city in a *palki*. After a great deal of proposals going back and forth, the king and queen at last consented to the proposal.[1]

The party came to the outskirts of the weaver's village; the palki bearers were sent away; and the princess, who asked where her husband's palace was, was made to walk on foot. The weaver's hut was soon reached.

The jackal, addressing the princess, said, "This, madam, is your husband's palace."

As there was nothing for it, the princess soon got reconciled to her fate. She, however, determined to make her husband rich, especially as she knew the secret of becoming rich. One day she told her husband to get for her a pice-worth of flour. She put a little water in the flour and smeared her body with the paste. When the paste dried on her body, she began wiping the paste with her fingers; and as the paste fell in small balls from her body, it got turned into gold. She repeated this process every day for some time, and thus got an immense quantity of gold. She soon became mistress of more gold than is to be found in the coffers of any king. With this gold she employed a whole army of masons, carpenters and architects, who in no time built one of the finest palaces in the world.

The princess can only be the goddess Lakshmi, who is the goddess of every kind of wealth – material and spiritual. As a pice

---

[1] As a Palki is a type of palanquin or sedan chair used by devotees for carrying a Guru from place to place, it is quite likely that the weaver in the original story had become a guru due to the tasks he had accomplished. This would explain the term 'incognito' because a guru is still a very distinguished person in India and is treated with a great deal of pomp and ceremony- in Vedic Russia it was presumably even greater.

is a small coin of very little value, she has performed a miracle of making an abundance of gold from very little. But the greatest wealth is the spiritually transformed mind and body of the weaver of Patanjali's sutras.

Seven hundred families of weavers were sought for and settled round about the palace.

As we said in the beginning, all of the seven hundred families of weavers would be advanced spiritual initiates, whose presence would produce a heightened feeling of peace and well-being and also render that area totally safe from any kind of attack.

After this, she wrote a letter to her father to say that she was sorry he had not favoured her with a visit since the day of her marriage, and that she would be delighted if he now came to see her and her husband. The king agreed to come, and a day was fixed. The princess made great preparations for the day of her father's arrival.

Hospitals were established in several parts of the town for diseased, sick and infirm animals. The beasts in thousands were given betel leaves to chew by the wayside.

The streets were covered with cashmere shawls for her father and his attendants to walk on. There was no end of the display of wealth and grandeur. The king and queen arrived in state, and were infinitely delighted at the apparently boundless riches of their son-in-law.

The jackal once again appeared on the scene. He saluted the king and queen and said, "Didn't I tell you?"

The 25% intelligence of the weaver had been transformed back to 100%. The miserable hut was once again a beautiful palace, comparable to those of his famed ancestors.

The Flying Ship

Introduction

It is interesting to note that this is a Russian version of two of the Grimm brothers' stories, *How Six Men Got on in the World* and *The Six Servants*. Even more interesting is that all three stories feature the siddhi techniques of the Yoga Sutras of Patanjali.

Once upon a time, there lived an old peasant and his wife. They had three sons. The two eldest were clever. The old woman loved them. She cooked them tasty dishes and laundered their clothes but the youngest, whose name was Ivan, was dirty and was considered a fool.

The secret aim of many so-called 'fairy tales' was for a spiritual master or guru to compose an easy story to remember, written in a code that any of his followers could easily decipher whilst appearing to be a tall story that everybody else could enjoy. Not only was this a useful tool for the seeker's spiritual growth , but it also had the double advantage of protecting him from persecution by despotic regimes enforcing a different religion, in which any real connection to the god within would be forbidden in the Dwarpa and Kali Yuga periods of time. This would be when the world is far away from its source in Brahma loka and the average understanding falls by 50% or more.

As in other stories using this code, the hero and his family are different aspects of the same person. Thus, his brothers are his senses and mind. His mother would be the ever-changing field of relative creation and the father, his ego. Ivan, being the youngest and least worldly, was his buddhi or spiritualised intellect.

One day the Tsar had sent heralds to announce that he wanted a flying ship to be built. Whoever built it would have the hand of his daughter in marriage, as well as half his kingdom.

In most Russian stories, the Tsar, as head of state was originally equated with God. In this one also this was probably the case originally, so here 'half the kingdom' would mean to have an equal share in God's estate – namely the unmanifest absolute and relative creation.

It is very hard to believe they could build a space ship in the distant past but there certainly was such a time. One of the rishis who cognised some of the hymns of the Veda *was named Bharadvaja. He was not only a great Vedic seer, but also a great aeronautics engineer who wrote a treatise on space ships called 'Vimanas' and how to propel them safely through space. However, that is not the true intent of this tale.*

The two eldest brothers decided to try their luck and build such a ship. Their mother baked them tarts and roasted chicken and goose to have on their journey and gave them her blessing.

The brothers went to the forest and began to chop trees. They chopped many branches and didn't know what to do afterwards. They started to abuse each other and suddenly noticed an old man standing nearby.

"Why are you scolding each other?" he asked.

"Go away, beggar!" replied the brothers. Some time later the brothers went back home.

A few days after, Ivan begged his parents for permission to try his luck too.

The youngest son or daughter in these wisdom tales is always the buddhi and therefore the least worldly aspect of the mind. Because they always see things in a different and more coherent way and always listen to the advice of their inner selves, they sometimes look stupid in the eyes of the worldly. Thus in reality, Ivan was actually very advanced on the path of spirituality. He was well on the path to take to the air himself, without the aid of a flying ship.

"You will never be able to make such a journey and will probably be eaten by wild animals on the way," said his mother.

The youngest was insistent on his decision and started his journey. His mother gave him a thick slice of stale bread and sent him on his way.

Ivan went to the forest, to fell a tall Siberian Cedar pine tree to begin building the flying ship. The old man came to him and asked: "What are you doing here?"

"I want to build the flying ship," replied Ivan.

"It's difficult to build such a ship," added the old man.

"Old people are wise," stated Ivan. "Can you show me how to do it?"

The old man instructed Ivan how he should build the flying ship within himself and enabled Ivan to build it with great ease. The old man praised Ivan for his good work and offered him to have a snack.

The old man was obviously either the inner atman or somebody wise in the knowledge of his ancestors in Vedic times. He would have known it was a big mistake to think that flying ship could be made by felling a such a remarkable tree , when the benefits of its oil, cones and properties of a living tree far out-weigh its value as timber. The Siberian Sage Anastasia tells us that the rhythms and pulsations of the ringing cedars are close to the great intelligence of the creator. It is possible for a person to place their hand on the warm trunk of a ringing cedar tree and communicate with the infinite expanse of wisdom.

What the old man was actually giving him was the knowledge of how to attain the turiya state and the flying sutra of the Yoga Sutras of Patanjali.

"I can only offer you stale bread," said Ivan sadly. "It's disgusting!"

The stale bread that was all Ivan had to offer represents what knowledge and beliefs he had learned from relative creation.

"Don't worry about that," replied the old man. "I can soon fix that."

Ivan gave him bread and with a few words in an archaic language, the old man turned it into freshly baked wheat bread as soon as he touched it. After the meal the old man gave Ivan some instructions:

"You should take on board every wayfarer you pass!"

The few words in an archaic language were almost certainly how to pronounce the Patanjali sutras for super-normal powers in Sanskrit.

Meaning accept whatever naturally comes your way innocently and without doubt. He was probably referring to the eight psychic perfections. They are as follows:

1/ Anima – the yogi can make themselves as small as an atom

2/ Mahima – the body can be made infinitely large

3/ Laghima – the body can be made lighter than air

4/ Garima – the body can be made to come very heavy

5/ Prapti – is the ability to reach anywhere

6/ Prakmya – is the ability to fulfil any desire without obstructions

7/ Vashitva – gives one control over all objects – organic or inorganic

8/ Ishitva – is the ability to create or destroy at will

Ivan thanked the old man profusely. No sooner did he sit down in the ship than it rose up into the air, soaring high above the treetops, the rivers and the wide fields.

In India, the human body is still regarded by realized gurus as a boat that enables one to cross the ever-changing sea of samsara to become anchored to the unchanging, transcendental field of the absolute.

As he flew along, he spied a man below, kneeling on the ground with his ear pressed to the earth. Ivan was very surprised and asked the man: "What are you doing with your ear pressed to the ground?"

"I am listening to how birds are singing in the distant Southlands. I can hear all that is happening, no matter where in the world it is," answered the man.

As well as acquiring the flying sutra, the sutra for divine hearing enters into Ivan's mind. Sound travels through the finest of the five elements called akasha, which has not yet been found by modern science yet. By practising samyama on the organ of hearing and its relationship to the akasha, it is possible to gain access to the super physical sounds. There are four aspects of sound: the physical, the audible, mental and transcendental. We are used to the idea of our sense of sound being restricted to a certain range, whereas even cats and dogs exceed our capabilities.

The ability to hear sound beyond our restricted range can be gradually developed. However, when a sound goes beyond our normal range it does not stop – it continues in a more subtle or attenuated form. Divine hearing is the process of becoming sensitive to sounds before they fade away in the stillness of the transcendental state. In fact, Maharishi's technique of transcendental meditation is based upon this principle.

"Come and join me in my flying ship!" exclaimed Ivan.

The man agreed, climbed on board and they flew into the blue sky. They had not flown far when they saw a man hopping on one leg with the other tied to his ear. Ivan demanded of him: "Why are you hopping on one foot with the other tied to your ear?"

"If I don't do it, I will step across the world in no time at all," replied the man.

"Then come and join us in my flying ship!" offered Ivan, bringing the ship down to land. The man on one foot hopped into the ship and off they flew again.

The ability to run faster than birds can fly is likely to be the fifth of the eight psychic perfections. It is called prapti and gives one the ability to reach anywhere.

Over forest and meadow they flew, until they noticed a man shooting his gun at nothing at all in the sky. Ivan brought his ship down and asked the man why he was aiming his gun at the sky when there was not a bird in sight.

"I am aiming my gun at the greyhen, which is sitting on the tree situated at a distance of a thousand kilometres from here," answered the man.

In the original story, this was the figurative ploy for obtaining the full refinement of the sense of sight. The story only refers to seeing a long way at the gross level, but the full development of the sense of sight would entail the ability to examine visually every level of creation from the cosmic to the sub-atomic.

"Come and join us!" said Ivan.

When he was on board, Ivan cast off. On and on they sailed through the endless sky until they saw a man below carrying a sack full of loaves on his back. Ivan steered the ship until it was level with the man and asked:

"Where are you going with such a load?"

"I am going to town to get bread for my dinner," answered the man.

Ivan was puzzled and exclaimed: "But you have a whole sack full of loaves on your back!"

"That's nothing. I could swallow that in one gulp and still be hungry," replied the man.

The Hungry Man reminds me of the Norse god Loki, who was noted for having an enormous appetite for food and an equally infinite capacity to store it. By food, it means food of the mind, body and senses of everything in creation. In terms of the eight perfections, the huge appetite of the hungry man is a personification of Patanjali's 'mahima', the yogi's ability to make their body very large – in other words become one with the purusha aspect, the whole of creation.

"Come and join us!" called Ivan, landing the ship beside the Hungry Man, who accepted the offer.

As soon as he climbed aboard they soared off. They had not gone far when they saw a man walking round and round a lake.

Ivan asked him: "Why are you walking round the lake?"

"I feel thirsty, but I can find no water," answered the man.

"But there is a whole lake of water in front of you!" said Ivan.

"I could swallow this lake in one gulp and still go thirsty," replied the man.

Similarly, water is an allegory for 'taste' in its widest sense. Whilst the previous example related to the hunger of unfulfilled desire, taste is its fruition. In fact, the purpose of meditation is to offer up one's unfulfilled desires to the transcendent. When the mind transcends it brings a supreme rest to the body, which awakens an unfulfilled desire in the form of a thought, but instead of enjoying the thought in its entirety one overrides it by going back to the mantra. This is how one eventually frees oneself from the karma load one brings into the world.

Ivan invited the Thirsty Man to join his voyage and he climbed on board.

On they flew until they saw a man walking into a forest with a bundle of brushwood on his back.

"Why are you taking brushwood into the forest?" asked Ivan.

"This is not just ordinary brushwood. I only have to scatter it over the plain and a whole army will spring up," the man replied. He also stepped on to the ship.

This could be any one of the three particular psychic perfections but it is most likely to be Ishitva, the ability to destroy or create at will.

Shortly afterwards they met a man carrying a bale of hay. But this was no ordinary hay. No matter how hot the sun shone, he only had to spread the hay upon the ground and a cool breeze would spring up and snow and frost would follow. He was the last wayfarer to join the band in the ship.

This ability is called the mastery of the bhutas, which confers on a person control over the five elements of earth, water, fire, air and space or akasha from their finest to their gross forms of manifestation. It would also give that person the ability to balance an excess of any element with another.

They continued their journey and soon they reached the royal courtyard. At that time the Tsar was having his breakfast. Seeing the flying ship most visitors were astonished. The servants told him that common peasants had arrived and there wasn't a single person of noble blood.

The royal courtyard would be the finest essence of the source of creation. Ivan's comrades would be the perfections of the mind, body and senses.

The Tsar was extremely displeased. How could he possibly allow his daughter to marry a simple peasant? He asked his boyars to help him and they gave him the following advice: "You should set impossible tasks for these peasants and then you will be able to get rid of them without going back on your word."

In fact God would not be displeased but it is natural to set a devotee tasks.

So the Tsar ordered Ivan to bring him two jugs: a jug of the Water of Life and a jug of the Water of Death – and to bring them to him before he had finished eating his breakfast! Ivan was shocked because he couldn't fulfil this order.

As one can see these are figurative tasks that would be well beyond any human tsar.

The one they called Giantsteps said: "Don't worry, I will bring the jugs in a minute!".

He unhitched his leg from his ear, ran to the remote kingdom and collected the jugs. Then he thought to himself: "I have plenty of time so it is possible to have a rest." He sat under a big oak and dozed off. Back at the palace, the Tsar was just finishing his breakfast and the men in the flying ship were becoming uneasy.

The first wayfarer (the one who could hear the slightest sound near and far) put his ear to the ground and heard the mighty snores of Giantsteps beneath the big oak. The Marksman took his gun and fired at the oak. Acorns fell on the head of Giantsteps and woke him. Giantsteps jumped up and brought the water in several seconds.

The Tsar looked at the jugs of the Water of Life and the Water of Death and decided to test the magic water. Servants caught a cock and splashed the Water of Death on it. The cock died at once. Then the servant splashed the Water of Life on it and the cock returned to life.

There are several accounts of 'the water of life' in the Bible*: John 4:14 says 'whoever drinks of the water that I will give him shall never thirst; but the water that I will give him will become in him a well of water springing up to eternal life.'*

Another is Revelation 22:1-2: 'Then he showed me a river of the water of life, clear as crystal, coming from the throne of God and of the Lamb, in the middle of its street. On either side of the river was the tree of life, bearing twelve kinds of fruit, yielding its fruit every month; and the leaves of the tree were for the healing of the nations.'

Both are the fruits of a ripened spiritual seeker seeking union with God; they do not exist on the relative field of life as objects one can fetch and carry.

In Eastern philosophy things are much clearer. Firstly there is no death. It is true that the body wears out but that is just like the pattern of the day – after a period of activity comes a period of rest. Following that, when the time is right, we can continue on the path of liberation by acquiring another body.

In the subtle body are three main nerve channels called nadis. Two of them support our gross body during our life on earth. These are figuratively named after the three main rivers in India – namely the Ganges, the Yumana and the hidden Saraswati. The latter is the actual river of life called the kundalini. When it rises to penetrate and unify the other two the spiritual baptism into eternal life occurs.

Foiled on the first task, the Tsar set a second. This time it was even more impossible: to eat a dozen roast oxen and a dozen freshly baked loaves in a single sitting. Ivan groaned:

"I could not eat a single ox in a week!"

It is at this point that the whole point of the story has been forgotten and thus misinterpreted through the ages. What was originally meant here were the excellent rewards of the aforesaid unity would have been equal to having inwardly digested the qualities of a dozen oxen. In the agrarian times when this tale was composed the ox was man's best friend. It was strong, gentle and vigilant – in fact the perfect animal.

Historically, the ox was invaluable because of the work it did, such as pulling the plough or carriage and transporting goods from one place to another. A proverb that has survived to modern times is: a man without land is half a pauper but one without an ox is a complete pauper.

Apparently slavonic peasants called their oxen 'angels' and addressed them as 'father' or 'brother'.

Finally, an ox was not put to death when it grew too old to work. Oxen were allowed to roam free in the fields and die a natural death. They were buried with every respect due to them.

There is still a remnant of their attitude to Oxen that has survived in Bulgaria. There are a number of feast days on which the health of oxen is still celebrated in Bulgaria –St. Sylvester, St. Vlas and St. Modest. On Christmas Eve a special ritual loaf is baked in the shape of a ploughman with his oxen.

This would be the original meaning of the twelve loaves Ivan had to eat.

The Hungry Man calmed Ivan and said: "Don't worry, that is only enough to whet my appetite!" With that the Hungry Man devoured the twelve roast oxen and twelve freshly baked loaves in one gulp – and then called for more!

The Tsar was furious. He called for forty pails of beer to be poured into each of forty barrels and commanded that all this was to be consumed in a single draught.

Again Ivan was crestfallen. But the Thirsty Man cheered him up: "I can drain them all in one draught, and still have room for more!"

And so it was.

This time the Tsar was desperate. He gave orders for an iron bathhouse to be heated until it was white hot. The Tsar ordered Ivan to spend the night steaming himself in it. "That would surely put an end to him," the Tsar thought to himself.

Ivan entered the bathhouse in the company of the Straw Man, who scattered his hay across the iron floor. This made the temperature drop so slowly that Ivan had barely washed himself before the water turned to ice. When the Tsar unlocked the bathhouse the next morning, Ivan stepped out, washed and clean and as fresh as a daisy!

Another consequence of unifying the three nadis is that transcendental consciousness coexists with the waking state. Thus it is possible to unify two emotions that previously would have been strongly opposed to each other. In this case it is actually an example of unifying the two extreme emotions of hot and cold. I had a similar experience during a boat ride in Allahabad. I found myself to be crying and laughing at the same time. To be quite honest I didn't know what it all meant, until the goddess revealed the truth. She said I had united the two extreme emotions of joy and sadness.

The Tsar was beside himself with rage. He commanded Ivan to assemble an entire regiment of troops by the next morning. At last he had found the best solution to the entire problem, for from where could a simple peasant raise an army? He would then be rid of Ivan once and for all!

The path to cosmic consciousness is one of purifying the mind. Beyond this major milestone is the path to God consciousness, which purifies the emotions.

Ivan was distressed because he couldn't complete this order. The Brushwood suddenly exclaimed: – "You have forgotten me! I can raise a whole host of fighting men in the twinkle of an eye.

And if the Tsar refuses to give up his daughter after that, our army will conquer his kingdom!"

In the morning Ivan and his friend went in the field and spread brushwood over the grass and in the twinkling of an eye a vast army of cavalry, infantry and artillery appeared.

When the Tsar awoke the next morning and saw the army before his palace, with banners and pennants fluttering in the morning breeze, he took fright and ordered his generals to withdraw the royal army- Ivan burst into the palace. The Tsar was very frightened, so he grovelled at Ivan's feet, asking him to marry his daughter.

Again – the modern storyteller is way off track because the unification of the three major nadis is also called a marriage.

The great Lord Shankara said: "If Shiva is united with Shakti, he is able to create. If he is not, he is incapable even of stirring."

This is because Shakti is the embodiment of energy and dynamism, and the motivating force behind all action and existence in the material universe. Shiva is her transcendent masculine aspect, providing the divine ground of all being. "There is no Shiva without Shakti, or Shakti without Shiva. The two [...] in themselves are One." (It is a quote from the first line of a poem called Saundarya by the great sage Adi Shankara 800CE.)

Ivan said: "I won't obey you any more!"

We can only infer that the Tsar in this aspect was the ego, opposed to the entire law of dharma.

Ivan turned the Tsar out of the kingdom and married the princess. No one ever referred to Ivan as 'the Fool' after that. He became a clever ruler who was fair to common people. Everybody loved and respected him, especially the princess, with whom he lived happily for the rest of his days.

Tsarevich Ivan and Grey Wolf

Introduction

The aim of restoring elements of these stories as they were originally set out is vital because a new and better age will soon be here. One can only do the best one can with the information that is available at the time. Without great teachers like Maharishi, we would be led to take it for granted that the names of Tsars denoted different kingdoms of a country on earth, when in actual fact the masters who originally composed these tales were speaking about the sequence of spiritual modifications of the mind and emotions of an individual person by giving him access to the turiya state, which is the actual transforming agent that eventually unites him with God. So it is not surprising that fairy tales often end with 'they all lived happily ever after'.

Thus every time we read that Tsarevich Ivan was quiet before the next part of his spiritual quest, he was far from sad; he was enjoying the bliss of suffusing his mind with transcendental bliss consciousness. This unifies mental and emotional opposites into a neutral state in which both are able to co-exist peacefully. This is the significance of Grey Wolf. Grey is a neutral balance between black and white. Thus he symbolises the organising power beyond the worldly opposites. He combines all the affections and tolerances of our favourite animal friend with a fundamental knowledge about everything in creation.

This is the Russian version of the Grimm brothers' *The Golden Bird*, as well as many other variants in Slav nations. There appear to be similar versions all around the world, as per Aarne-Thompson 550.

TSAREVICH IVAN AND GREY WOLF

Once upon a time there was a Tsar named Berendei, and he had three sons, the youngest of whom was called Ivan.

The name of the Tsar is an important clue, as in most tales all the characters in the story are either aspects or developments of the same person. Wikipedia tells us that Berendei is a Slavic male given name derived from the Old Norse name Guðleifr, which means "heir of god". It is popular in Russia. It is also commonly used in Ukraine.

Now the Tsar had a beautiful garden with an apple tree in it which bore golden apples.

The Tsar in this case is the formless, all-knowing absolute. His or her garden is the sphere of relative creation, which could be called the sphere of becoming.

The unnamed fruit of Eden thus became an apple, due to the influence of the Greek myth of the golden apples in the Garden of Hesperides. This resulted in the apple becoming a symbol for knowledge, immortality, temptation, the fall of humans and sin.

In a wider context the apple tree is also associated with virtue. Both the tree and its fruit are symbols of purity and motherhood.

It corresponds to the sahasrara, which is situated at the crown of the head and is often called the seventh chakra, which connects us with the universe and the divine source of creation. That is why it symbolises immortality and unity.

One day the Tsar discovered that somebody was visiting his garden and stealing his golden apples. The Tsar was very unhappy about this. He sent watchmen into the garden, but they were unable to catch the thief. The Tsar was so grieved that he would not touch food or drink. His sons tried to cheer him.

"Do not grieve, Father dear," they said, "we shall keep watch over the garden ourselves."

The eldest son said: "Today it is my turn to keep watch."

As in other stories, the two more worldly sons are his senses and mind, whereas his youngest son Ivan is the more inward-looking buddhi or spiritualised intellect.

And he went into the garden. He walked about for a long time but saw no one, so he flung himself down on the soft grass and went to sleep.

In the morning the Tsar said to him: "Come, now, have you brought me good news? Have you discovered who the thief is?"

"No, Father dear. That the thief was not there, I am ready to swear. I did not close my eyes all night, but I saw no one."

This aspect of him was called Dmitri – meaning earth lover or the love of the external pleasures of the earth. His eyes would not be open wide to observe a spiritual event, especially if it was out of tune with mainstream thought.

On the following night the middle son went out to keep watch, and he, too, went to sleep and in the morning said he had seen no one. It was now the youngest son's turn to go and keep watch.

This aspect of him was Vasili. People with that name are known to be very business-minded and good at making money – not a good candidate for reporting a religious experience, so he went to sleep instead.

Tsarevich Ivan went to watch his father's garden and he did not dare so much as to sit down, let alone lie down. If he felt that he was getting sleepy, he would wash his face in dew and become wide awake again. Half the night passed by, and all of a sudden what should he see but a light shining in the garden.

Brighter and brighter it grew, and it lit up everything around. Tsarevich Ivan looked, and there in the apple-tree he saw the firebird pecking at the golden apples. Tsarevich Ivan crept up to the tree and caught the bird by the tail. But the firebird broke free of his grasp and flew away, leaving a feather from its tail in his hand. In the morning Tsarevich Ivan went to his father.

On the other hand, Tsarevich Ivan was just the right person for the job. In meditation he experienced the movement of the kundalini up his spine, often called the spiritual firebird. The feather from its tail would be a token to show that he had achieved a more advanced state which Maharishi calls cosmic consciousness. He regards it as the first advanced state of awareness and the foundation for the higher states of consciousness to follow.

"Well, my son, have you caught the thief?" asked the Tsar.

"No, Father," said Tsarevich Ivan, "I have not caught him, but I have discovered who he is. See, he sends you this feather as a keepsake. The firebird is the thief, Father."

The Tsar took the feather, and from that time he became cheerful again and began to eat and drink. But one fine day he fell to thinking about the firebird and, calling his sons to his side, said: "My dear sons, I would have you saddle your trusty steeds and set out to see the wide world. If you search in all its far corners, perhaps you will come upon the firebird."

Once one has experienced the initiation into cosmic consciousness, it vastly changes one's view of the world and leads one to seek for more. It is transcendental consciousness co-existing with the waking state. It signifies that the purity of the mind has been achieved.

The sons bowed to their father, saddled their trusty steeds and set out. The eldest son took one road, the middle son another, and Tsarevich Ivan a third.

Whether Tsarevich Ivan was long on the way or not, no one can say, but one day, it being summer and very warm, he felt so tired that he got off his horse and, binding its feet so that it could not go very far, lay down to rest. Whether he slept for a long time or a little time nobody knows, but when he woke up he found that his horse was gone. He went to look for it, he walked and he walked, and at last he found its remains: nothing but bones, picked clean.

Tsarevich Ivan was greatly grieved. How could he continue on his journey without a horse?

"Ah, well," he thought, "it cannot be helped, and I must make the best of it." And he went on foot. He walked and walked till he was so tired that he was ready to drop. He sat down on the soft grass, and he felt very sad and woebegone.

Suddenly, lo and behold! Who should come running up to him but Grey Wolf.

The next step after achieving cosmic consciousness is to achieve contact with one's inner guide, which is called the atman. The atman can take any form – initially it is one that will suit the seeker best. This opens up an amazingly new vista of life because the atman knows everything about what is taking place in the material world at any time and guides one's journey through life accordingly.

"Why are you sitting here so sad and sorrowful, Tsarevich Ivan?" asked Grey Wolf.

As the next step on one's spiritual journey is the refinement of the emotions, leading to God Consciousness, it is fitting that the original composer of the tale chose people's best friend to symbolise the supreme inner spiritual guide. In the Grimm brothers' version it was a fox, in this version it is a wolf. Not just any wolf, but a grey one. Grey is a unification of the extreme colours black and white. It is a mature and responsible colour that is associated with deep wisdom of one who has lived a long time and has seen it all. From my own experience – one's inner guide knows everything. Her knowledge isn't just on a religious or academic level, she knows which is the best shop to go to for a particular item and also the best route not to be held up by traffic. Last but not least is the state of ever-growing love between one's ishta devata and oneself. In fact it is called the path of devotion.

Before waking up to one's inner guide, everybody we meet, every situation we have encountered through life, seems to be authored by ourselves: but actually we were taken there by our silent inner guide. Before reaching cosmic consciousness we use our free will, so whatever action we take is up to us. If it is in accord with the laws of dharma we will be rewarded, but if it is not we will be punished.

At this point in life when we become aware of our atman, the position is reversed. Whereas our ishta was our vehicle that took us to every next encounter, now he or she is in charge and we become his or her vehicle to carry out whatever he or she wants us to do in this dimension. So from that time on the celestial dimension is in charge and we become one of their messengers to help improve the world by carrying out the tasks our istha devata sets.

"How can I help being sad, Grey Wolf? I have lost my trusty steed."

"It was I who ate up your horse, Tsarevich Ivan. But I am sorry for you. Come, tell me, what are you doing so far from home and where are you going?"

The horse he was referring to was Tsarevich Ivan's free will as an individual.

"My father has sent me out into the wide world to seek the firebird."

"Has he now? Well, you could not have reached the firebird on that horse in three years. I alone know where it lives. So be it – since I have eaten up your horse, I shall be your true and faithful servant. Get on my back and hold fast."

Tsarevich Ivan got on his back and Grey Wolf was off in a flash. Blue lakes skimmed past ever so fast, green forests swept by in the wink of an eye, and at last they came to a castle with a high wall round it.

"Listen carefully, Tsarevich Ivan," said Grey Wolf, "and remember what I say. Climb over that wall. You have nothing to fear –we have come at a lucky hour, all the guards are sleeping. In a chamber within the tower you will see a window, in that window hangs a golden cage, and in that cage is the firebird. Take the bird and hide it in your bosom, but mind you do not touch the cage!"

The 'lucky hour' is called a sandhi – normally dawn, noon or dusk – which is a very good time to meditate. In meditation the waking state will be on hold. The tower is the path the kundalini takes as it climbs the nadi within the spine to where the firebird is situated in the head. However, if the attention strays away from the mantra the waking state returns.

Tsarevich Ivan climbed over the wall and saw the tower with the golden cage in the window and the firebird in the cage. He took the bird out and hid it in his bosom, but he could not tear his eyes away from the cage.

"Ah, what a handsome golden cage it is!" he thought longingly. "How can I leave it here?" And he forgot all about the Wolf's warning. But the moment he touched the cage, a hue and cry arose within the castle – trumpets began to blow, drums began to beat, and the guards woke up, seized Tsarevich Ivan and marched him off to Tsar Afron.

Once again Tsarevich Ivan succumbed to the temptations of the external world, quite forgetting his true mission. What actually happened was that Tsarevich experienced a thought in his meditation, which led him away from his goal. He followed the thought instead of going back to the mantra and transcending again.

"Who are you and whence do you hail?" Tsar Afron demanded angrily.

"I am Tsarevich Ivan, son of Tsar Berendei."

"Fie, shame on you! To think of the son of a tsar being a thief!"

"Well, you should not have let your bird steal apples from our garden."

"If you had come and told me about it in an honest way, I would have made you a present of the firebird out of respect for your father, Tsar Berendei. But now I shall spread the ill fame of your family far and wide. Or no – perhaps I will not, after all. If you do what I tell you, I shall forgive you.

In a certain tsardom there is a Tsar named Kusman and he has a horse with a golden mane. Bring me that horse and I will make you a gift of the firebird and the cage besides."

This aspect of dharma or natural law is called Kusman. Rather like the outcomes of Afron, they are dramatically different. The results of our actions either bring great success or abject misery. However, as before our ishta always gives us the opportunity to moderate by giving service to others and not pursuing the path of self-glorification.

The golden horse with the golden mane is the energy that drives creation and the bridle gives one control of it. Kusman is the fourth of the nine names of Durga. It shows that the entire universe from the smallest atom is under her control and direction.

Tsarevich Ivan felt very sad and crestfallen, and he went back to Grey Wolf.

"I told you not to touch the cage," said the Wolf. "Why did you not heed my warning?"

"I am sorry, Grey Wolf, please forgive me."

"You are sorry, are you? Oh, well, get on my back again. I gave my word, and I must not go back on it. A truth that all good folk accept is that a promise must be kept."

And off went Grey Wolf with Tsarevich Ivan on his back. Whether they travelled for a long or a little time nobody knows, but at last they came to the castle where the horse with the golden mane was kept.

"Climb over the wall, Tsarevich Ivan, the guards are asleep," said Grey Wolf. "Go to the stable and take the horse, but mind you do not touch the bridle."

Tsarevich Ivan climbed over the castle wall and, all the guards being asleep, he went to the stable and caught the horse with the golden mane. But he could not help picking up the bridle. It was made of gold and set with precious stones, a fitting bridle for such a horse. No sooner had Tsarevich Ivan touched the bridle than a hue and cry was raised within the castle. Trumpets began to blow, drums began to beat, and the guards woke up, seized Tsarevich Ivan and marched him off to Tsar Kusman.

A similar thing to what had happened previously made Tsarevich Ivan forget to go back to the mantra, with the result that he was transported back to all the noise and clamour of the waking state.

"Who are you and whence do you hail?" the Tsar demanded.

"I am Tsarevich Ivan."

"A tsar's son stealing horses! What a foolish thing to do! A common peasant would not stoop to it. But I shall forgive you, Tsarevich Ivan, if you do what I tell you. Tsar Dalmat has a daughter named Yelena the Fair. Steal her and bring her to me, and I shall make you a present of my horse with the golden mane and of the bridle besides."

So the next aspect of natural law is dalmat. A person displaying the disposition of dalmat finds the best contentment in life is looking after one's home and family. Such a person has a great sense of responsibility and duty. Their nature is to be comforting, appreciative and affectionate.

Gold always symbolises pure spirituality, in much the same way as Sat yuga is the golden age with the longest duration in each 12,000 year yuga.

Tsarevich Ivan felt more sad and crestfallen than ever, and he went back to Grey Wolf.

"I told you not to touch the bridle, Tsarevich Ivan!" said the Wolf. "Why did you not heed my warning?"

"I am sorry, Grey Wolf, please forgive me."

"Being sorry won't do much good. Oh, well, get on my back again."

And off went Grey Wolf with Tsarevich Ivan. By and by they came to the tsardom of Tsar Dalmat, and in the garden of his castle Yelena the Fair was strolling with her women and maids.

"This time I shall do everything myself," said Grey Wolf. "You go back the way we came and I will soon catch up with you."

Maharishi tells us that the final part of our quest called unity consciousness is carried out for us. It happens automatically.

So Tsarevich Ivan went back the way he had come, and Grey Wolf jumped over the wall into the garden. Ivan crouched behind a bush and peeped out, and his heart leapt with joy, for there was Grey Wolf with Yelena the Fair on his back!

The beautiful Yelena was symbolic of the full development of the heart in God Consciousness.

"You get on my back too, and be quick about it, or they may catch us," said Grey Wolf. Grey Wolf sped down the path with Tsarevich Ivan and Yelena the Fair on his back. Blue lakes skimmed past ever so fast, green forests swept by in the wink of an eye.

Whether they were long on the way or not nobody knows, but by and by they came to Tsar Kusman's tsardom.

The main clue here is the meaning of the tsar of this region's name. Kusman means the cosmos in all of its totality.

"Why are you so silent and sad, Tsarevich Ivan?" asked Grey Wolf.

"How can I help being sad, Grey Wolf! It breaks my heart to part with such loveliness. To think that I must exchange Yelena the Fair for a horse!"

"You need not part with such loveliness, we shall hide her somewhere. I will turn myself into Yelena the Fair and you shall take me to the Tsar instead."

So they hid Yelena the Fair in a hut in the forest, and Grey Wolf turned a somersault, and was at once changed into Yelena the Fair. Tsarevich Ivan took him to Tsar Kusman, and the Tsar was delighted and thanked him over and over again.

"Thank you for bringing me a bride, Tsarevich Ivan," said he. "Now the horse with the golden mane is yours, and the bridle too."

Tsarevich Ivan mounted the horse and went back for Yelena the Fair. He put her on the horse's back and away they rode! Tsar Kusman held a wedding and feast to celebrate it and he feasted the whole day long, and when bedtime came he led his bride into the bedroom. But when he got into bed with her what should he see but the muzzle of a wolf instead of the face of his young wife! So frightened was the Tsar that he tumbled out of bed, and Grey Wolf sprang up and ran away.

He caught up with Tsarevich Ivan and said: "Why are you sad, Tsarevich Ivan?"

"How can I help being sad! I cannot bear to think of exchanging the Horse with the Golden Mane for the firebird."

"Cheer up, I will help you," said the Wolf. Soon they came to the tsardom of Tsar Afron.

Once again, Afron, the name of the tsar of this particular area of being, is the clue to what this part of the story is really saying – it means 'the gift of God'.

"Hide the horse and Yelena the Fair," said the Wolf. "I will turn myself into Golden Mane and you shall take me to Tsar Afron."

So they hid Yelena the Fair and Golden Mane in the woods, and Grey Wolf turned a somersault and was changed into Golden Mane.

Tsarevich Ivan led him off to Tsar Afron, and the Tsar was delighted and gave him the firebird and the golden cage too. Tsarevich Ivan went back to the woods, put Yelena the Fair on Golden Mane's back and, taking the golden cage with the firebird in it, set off homewards.

Meanwhile Tsar Afron had the gift horse brought to him, and he was just about to get on its back when it turned into a grey wolf. So frightened was the Tsar that he fell down where he stood, and Grey Wolf ran away and soon caught up with Tsarevich Ivan.

"And now I must say goodbye," said he, "for I can go no further." Tsarevich Ivan got off the horse, bowed low three times, and thanked Grey Wolf humbly.

"Do not say goodbye for good, for you may still have need of me," said Grey Wolf.

"Why should I need him again?" thought Tsarevich Ivan. "All my wishes have been fulfilled." He got on Golden Mane's back and rode on with Yelena the Fair and the firebird.

This may well have been the end of the original story because what follows is a recap in another form of what has already been achieved.

By and by they reached Ivan's native land, and Tsarevich Ivan decided to stop for a bite to eat. He had a little bread with him, so they ate the bread and drank fresh water from the spring, and then lay down to rest. No sooner had Tsarevich Ivan fallen asleep than his brothers came riding up. They had been to other lands in search of the firebird, and were now coming home empty-handed.

When they saw that Tsarevich Ivan had got everything, they said: "Let us kill our brother Ivan, for then all his spoils will be ours." And with that they killed Tsarevich Ivan. Then they got on Golden Mane's back, took the firebird, seated Yelena the Fair on a horse and said: "See that you say not a word about this at home!"

So there lay Tsarevich Ivan on the ground, with the ravens circling over his head. All of a sudden who should come running but Grey Wolf. He ran up and he seized a raven and her fledgling.

"Fly and fetch me dead and living water, Raven," said the Wolf. "If you do, I shall let your nestling go."

The raven has been the mediator between birth and death in many cultures around the world so it is quite natural that he becomes the key to Tsarevich Ivan's future. As Kutkh he was supposed to have brought light, fire, language, fresh water, skills and copulation. In Indian philosophy it is the god Yama.

The Raven flew off – what else could she do? – while the Wolf held her fledgling. Whether a long time passed by or a little time nobody knows, but at last she came back with the dead and living water. Grey Wolf sprinkled the dead water on Tsarevich Ivan's wounds, and the wounds healed. Then he sprinkled him with the living water, and Tsarevich Ivan came back to life.

"Oh, how soundly I slept!" said he.

"Aye," said Grey Wolf, "and but for me you would never have wakened. Your own brothers killed you and took away all your treasures. Get on my back, quick."

They went off in hot pursuit, and they soon caught up the two brothers, and Grey Wolf tore them to bits and scattered the bits over the field. Tsarevich Ivan bowed to Grey Wolf and took leave of him for good.

While this makes sense in the later editions of the story the task was already completed. His brothers were his material attachments and unfulfilled desires in relative creation that normally keep one bound to the cycle of birth and death.

They were really the more primitive states of mind that would have been modified spiritually by the vivifying influence of the turiya state of Transcendental Consciousness, which finally transformed the Tsarevich from being 'the heir' of God to the state of Unity Consciousness, where he become One with God and creation.

He rode home on the horse with the golden mane, and he brought his father the firebird and himself a bride, Yelena the Fair.

Tsar Berendei was overjoyed and asked his son all about everything. Tsarevich Ivan told him how Grey Wolf had helped him, and how his brothers had killed him while he slept and Grey Wolf had torn them to bits.

At first Tsar Berendei was sorely grieved, but he soon got over it. And Tsarevich Ivan married Yelena the Fair and they lived together in health and cheer for many a long and prosperous year.

Post Script

Sometimes the answer to a question has been staring at us all the time – this is a case in point! Whilst the reasons I have given for the loss of understanding these stories are still possibly true, the main reason is obviously related to the decline in intelligence of mankind as the yugas descend from Satya, Treta, Dwapara and Kali Yuga.

I remember reading that Plato once said there are four levels of understanding. Firstly *mythos,* which is a wholly spiritual understanding and appreciation of the aim of life and all of our experiences. This is the norm for a person in Satya Yuga when people's understanding is at 100%.

The next is *dianoia,* when people's understanding falls by one quarter to 75%. This is an age when the role of religion becomes necessary and leaders prescribe methods to help the people to think and act effectively. By religion, we mean the ancient version of 'realigning with the truth' and not by blind faith and belief as it is understood today,

The third one down is *pistis,* meaning faith. At this level, thoughts and opinions are shaped by imitation. They are accepted on their face value from the ethos and shared values of the society in which life takes place in Dwarpara Yuga, not by direct experience or rigorous examination.

Finally, the grossest level of understanding is *eikasia,* which occurs in Kali Yuga. During that period of time the average intelligence falls to only 25% and people are totally absorbed by images, actions and events in the outside world.

Whilst we have heard or are aware of each of these characteristics in people's different levels of behaviour, our present age seems to be hovering in the junction point between Dwapara and Treta.

However, in addition, there is a chance of going back to 100%. Just as dawn and dusk are good times to meditate the period of time between one yuga and another is excellent for spiritual development.

Maharishi, who brought the system of transcendental meditation to the West, coined the phrase of 'restful alertness' to describe the turiya state and also to pinpoint its difference with other systems.

Maharishi's concept of 'restful alertness' is a crucial new experience to the mind and body, which has since been proven true scientifically The common understanding is that we are normally awake and alert in the waking state and in a restful state whilst asleep, but we have not experienced the two opposite aspects combined. Although we are nominally alert in the waking state, our degree of wakefulness is far from constant and it is our common experience to notice that it varies from day to day.

Maharishi's technique of transcendental meditation provides one with the ability to combine the two opposites each time we transcend and is a vital new experience for the mind and body. It allows the brain to witness how the organs of the body are supposed to interact and gradually improves the total coordination of the mind and body.

The restfulness causes deeply rooted stresses to unwind into thoughts but our mind is no longer captured by them. We just let them unwind. As soon as we realise we are back to thinking we return to the mantra, which takes us back to the transcendent again.

This repeated experience over a period of time allows us to free ourselves from the harmful stresses of the desires and aversions we have accumulated over many lifetimes and begin anew with the transcendent co-existing permanently with the waking state. This is what Maharishi calls cosmic consciousness, which is the foundation of the higher states of consciousness that are to follow, called God Consciousness and unity consciousness.

The original intention of the stories is borne out by the outcome of the ones we have just looked at – namely to realise contact with our inner divinity. When an opportunity for growth or solving a difficult problem in life comes your way, the best solution comes from within. Each dip into the pure consciousness of the turiya state adds a greater subtlety to our mental and emotional armoury, which allows us to deal with any situation in the outside world more comprehensively because our actions are more in tune with natural law. The more in tune with natural law we become, the greater becomes our wealth of happiness.

The goddess helped me to find the parts of the stories that changed the original intention of the composer and also altered the nature of the tale that was originally meant for an initiate.

Before we say goodbye, I want to impress upon you that I am not somebody special with unusual powers or abilities. I am just an ordinary old man. The only difference is that regular contact with the turiya state, which Maharishi calls transcendental consciousness, has refined my nervous system sufficiently to receive internal messages from the powers that actually administer the universe. In the West they are called angels; in India they are called devatas.

You have a nervous system similar to mine and have a whole array of special abilities lying latent within you. All you need do is to let your mind be refined by regular contact with the turiya state through Maharishi's easy, effortless, natural method of transcendental meditation. It is the perfect system for the busy lifestyle of modern life.

The second is not to expect or anticipate an overnight transformation but enjoy every new thing that is added to your life. Everything will come when the time is right.

The other thing to bear in mind that you are not being selfish by having a few minutes to yourself morning and evening – you are actually doing your bit to help the world become a better place. It will not only make life more pleasant at home but will also affect your local environment. The effects of the turiya state will be released into the world through whatever activity you are involved in and bring it that bit closer to the paradise it was designed to be.

In a golden age people are born with a whole array of *supernatural* abilities. They are still there within us in a sleepy form and need to be awakened through the infusion of pure consciousness.

If enough of us become enlightened a new golden age will be ushered in and everybody will live happily forever afterwards.

www.ingramcontent.com/pod-product-compliance
Lightning Source LLC
Chambersburg PA
CBHW050818090426
42737CB00021B/3426
* 9 7 8 1 8 3 9 7 5 0 8 7 8 *